FOR GODDESS' SAKE

FOR GODDESS' SAKE

Get the Girls Together and Have Some Fun

HAILEY D.D. KLEIN

CONARI PRESS

First published in 2004 by Conari Press,
an imprint of Red Wheel/Weiser, LLC
York Beach, ME
With offices at:
368 Congress Street, Boston, MA 02210
www.redwheelweiser.com

Library of Congress Cataloging-in-Publication Data

Klein, Hailey.
   For goddess' sake : get the girls together and have some fun /
Hailey D.D. Klein.
      p. cm.
Includes bibliographical references and index.
   ISBN 1-57324-914-9
   1. Women—Psychology. 2. Women—Conduct of life. 3. Goddess
religion. 4. Group relations training. I. Title.
HQ1206.K48 2004
305.4—dc22

2003023059

Typeset in Usherwood
Designed by Joyce C. Weston
Printed in Canada
TCP

11 10 09 08 07 06 05 04
      8 7 6 5 4 3 2 1

For my grandmothers:
Dolores DePierrefeu Daniels
and Maria Schick Klein Denhof

CONTENTS

CONTENTS

ACKNOWLEDGMENTS

This being my second book, I thought it might be easier somehow. Well, it wasn't. I did manage to keep my face to the sun for most of the ride though, and wouldn't trade a minute. Many thanks to those who fed and watered me along the way:

Jan Johnson, Michael Kerber, Robyn Heisey, Jill Rogers, and all the lovelies at Red Wheel/Weiser and Conari Press for bringing me with you and treating me so well. It's great to be back with ya'll.

The Passionistas for always saying Yes.

Marc Clopton and the Tuesday-night crew at the Actor's Studio in Newburyport for keeping me up at night in the throes of inspiration and delight and for helping me to hear the words "good work" in a profound new way.

Leslie Powell and Writers and Actors, INK for gentle wisdom and inspirational friendship.

Gareth Esersky, my agent, who keeps me blissfully ignorant of the hard parts I'm not good at and makes it all seem so easy.

The Goddesses for allowing me to tell our tales.

My dad for encouraging and supporting the notion that travel is an important part of an enriched life.

My sister Liz who is always in my corner even when I have so stubbornly backed myself into it.

My brother Joshua for reminding me when I am taking myself too seriously and for being almost funnier than me.

And to Lil, Whittles, and Magic for keeping me in all those wide open spaces.

FOR GODDESS' SAKE

INTRODUCTION

Soul is mingled in the whole.

—Aristotle

There you are. The girls and I were just thinking/talking about you. Pull up a chair, we have a lot to talk about.

The goddesses from long ago have never gone away. Even today, their stories continue to remind us of the lessons, strengths, and gifts they bestowed upon the world. Almost every culture has an ancient creation myth; the creator is usually a Great Mother or Great Goddess figure. She most often had the power to destroy as well as to create. Alas, as power structures changed and fear-based, aggressive leadership and governing became the norm, women were condemned for their reproductive and emotional powers. The reaction was to subjugate and repress, to strip women of as much influence as possible, to keep them under control and in line. We all know how well that works. When fear became the dominant motivator, persecution and mayhem ensued.

The Great Goddess was the pure representation of all

womankind *and* mankind—their lightness and dark, their strengths, vulnerabilities, and varying responses to situations and information, divine feminine energy. It was how societies figured out right from wrong. The Great Goddess exists in all of us today. She embodies every aspect of strength and wisdom, from physical to spiritual and practical as well. She is us at any given time—unpredictable, complex, curious, and holographic.

Living like a goddess involves embracing all of the goddess aspects that lie within each of us. When we are living curious, interactive, and joyful lives, we are accepting and loving of all our goddess qualities. *For Goddess' Sake* encourages you to acknowledge and affirm your goddess archetypes—the sexy girl, the damsel, the bruiser, the smartypants, the solo gal, the mystery woman, and more. Each one exists in every one of us. They show themselves at different times and in different circumstances. Throughout the book I encourage you to let them in.

We are usually focused on defining ourselves, or allowing others to define us, as only one aspect of ourselves at a time—nurturer, lover, sister, daughter, friend, caretaker, boss, coworker. We are all of those, and then some. No apologies or explanations necessary. Integration means accepting our complex selves as the whole, not just one piece, not just one aspect. Liberate yourself from constraint and restraint, and delve deep into all of your many layers.

GREAT GODDESS! IF THE SHOE FITS . . .

So if we are all Great Goddesses, what a fabulous group of gals we have to hang around with! Who comprehends us better than our friends in gender? Who cries with us when we get dumped or makes effigies of him and holds them over the coals? Who better understands our need to have lots and lots of toilet paper in the cupboard or a stash of chocolate in our sock drawer? Cinderella did the transformation thing to become a princess, but I always thought the stepsisters were a pretty interesting lot. Our conniving and creatively wicked sides are not something to shut out altogether; they're just another facet of the stone. I haven't come across too many complacent goddesses either. (I don't think the words *women* and *complacency* belong in the same sentence.)

The folks who understand this best are other women. Spending time in the company of other women is a wonderful way to remember and love all of our enchanting layers, attitudes, and emotions. If you have as many different facets as I do, you know that it takes patient and understanding gals to love and accept all fifty-seven of you. Revealing ourselves with other women is unique and sustaining.

Is there anything more energizing and uplifting than spending an evening with your favorite gal pals? There is laughter and acceptance and the ability to let go and just be women. It is inspiring and supportive. It is glorious. The energy exchange is dynamic and vibrant. And your women friends will always tell you they love your haircut or insist on reminding you that you are wonderful.

They can help you rediscover the Great Goddess that is within you. She is ready to support and teach you on this journey. She *is* you. We can invite her to the ball or leave Cinderella to languish at home. Be a good stepsister and invite her; you will all have a whole lot more fun. There are plenty of glass slippers to go around, but you may have to try on every pair of shoes. Not much of a hardship, I don't think.

Look out. Here comes a sidebar. I get distracted sometimes. Okay, often. I have lots to tell you so throughout the book you will see these thoughts that occur to me and that I feel compelled to pass along. They aren't always relevant to the previous paragraph but I hope they are interesting or at least provocative.

PEEL-OFF LABELS

None of the labels or descriptions women have been given are negative—none of them. Bitchy is not a bad thing to be sometimes, and neither is needy or sexy or wise. All of these parts

Glass Slippers

I was always annoyed in the Cinderella story that the stepsisters had big feet and couldn't fit into the teeny tiny glass slipper. Hrrrumph. If I didn't have my delightful size 10s, I would fall right over, well, more than I do already. Two of my best pals have size 6 feet, and it cracks me up when we go shoe shopping together. It is one of those wonderful times when I am struck by the variety of shapes and sizes that all of us glorious lady-belles come in. What a beautiful garden we are.

and pieces make us who we are and should be celebrated and nevermore shunned. And while we are at it, can we lose the labels and the categories and the putting ourselves and others in boxes, please! None of us can ever, ever be put in a category because we are nothing alike. We are each separate, complex, complicated, most glorious beings. Can't we just be who we are? We aren't broken and we don't need fixing. We aren't incomplete, and we aren't our mothers or our grandmothers or whoever they or anyone else tells us we are. We are whole right this minute, now and forever. Can you tell I feel strongly about this?

GODDESS SHMODDESS: WHO NEEDS ANOTHER GODDESS BOOK?

I hope you love this one. I hope you find this book a feast. Not only do I tell you all my trade secrets for putting together a goddess group and moving forward together, but I also bully you (in the most loving way, of course) into realizing that hanging around with other women can be a wicked awesome part of your spiritual practice—think of it as going to the gym and eating bon bons on the treadmill for your soul. We are talking about a treat for your insides—the airy, yearning, ethereal spirit part that needs love and attention. It is truly the part that matters most.

For Goddess' Sake assures women that the hunger to experience and participate in life to its fullest, to eat and drink in life and be madly merry is all part of the grand plan, and it shows you how. Garnished throughout with recipes to feed body and spirit, rituals and tasks to undertake with others or on your own, and a little dose of inspiration from ancient goddess lore the world over, this is the ultimate guide for women looking for a full, rich existence—to tap into energy, joy, and companionship, with themselves and with each other. Our fullness, joy, and acceptance of ourselves energizes the world like fistfuls of sparklers on a dark summer night.

We explore a variety of messages from goddesses throughout time, reminders of all that we are—an integration of the physical, spiritual, emotional, and intellectual. We can tap into any aspect at anytime. We are whole and complete every minute, and perfect as we are. We do not have to identify completely with an archetype in order to sense a glimmer of the familiar within ourselves. Glimmers of recognition are powerful catalysts toward thoughtful consideration of everything that we are and everything that we want to be. There are goddesses of war and love and home and hunting and on and on. Some are gentle, some bold, some vengeful, and others transformative. One goddess does not represent all women or the feminine divine in any culture. Why? Because forever ago it was realized and accepted that women are much more complex than that. We encompass many moods, emotions, strengths, and vulnerabilities. This is what we reclaim and celebrate here.

We don't have to define ourselves as one or two goddesses; we are a glorious collage of all these complex characters. Blend them, celebrate them, and embrace them all. Integrate and learn to love and appreciate all aspects of yourself as a woman.

WHY ME?

Who am I and why am I writing this book?

I have had a most extraordinary life thus far, with many adventures, encounters, careers, and revelations. I have been doing energy work, specifically Reiki, for more than ten years and love to create rituals with my clients and friends. I am privileged to be able to bring my energy work into the operating room, working with clients and several surgeons during pre-op, in surgery, and in post-op as a part of the healing team. I've worked behind the scenes in film and television and also with adolescents, and there have been many side roads taken in between. I used to worry that I had tried too many different paths or that maybe I should pick one. Not for me. All choices have led me right here to my second book.

I have enjoyed the benefits of belonging to a women's group for a decade. The company of these women continues to provide me with laughter, support, and nourishment of all kinds and I can't resist sharing some of our stories. I hope my words offer inspiration or comfort along the way. I don't even mind if my starry-eyed optimism drives you crazy—at least it's got you thinking.

I had written about my women's group before, extolling the joys of spending time with other women, reveling in their company and bearing witness to each other's lives. That was the spark that set *For Goddess' Sake* in motion. Here are the words that lit the flame:

> *I belong to a women's group. We call ourselves the god-desses—no disrespect or undue vanity intended. I don't even remember just how the name came about. We have been getting together faithfully once a month for six years; for dinner, laughter, conversation, and the chance to be just women for a few moments. Once a year or so we sneak away for a weekend to spend time outdoors at the ocean or in the woods. It isn't always easy for spouses and partners to understand the need we have for each other, the strength we gain from our connection and simply being together. We come back to them transformed each time, our spirits renewed, our wells refilled. One goddess' husband loves it when she has a weekend with the group because she always returns with a passionate appetite.*
>
> *We are artists, writers, businesswomen, teachers, mothers, wives, daughters, partners, married, divorced, single, employers, employees, and self-employed. We are thirty-something, forty-something and fifty-something—outdoorsy, indoorsy, dramatic, and shy. But when we come together each month, we are women. We need no other*

title. It is a refuge from expectations. It is the glory of no-strings-attached connecting with acceptance and love.

Each of us in the group has been lovingly carried through bumpy times. We have been mentored, cajoled, and lauded through brave change, confusion, new relationships, grief, loss, and triumph alike. The energy created by our connection is tremendous. We often joke that the estrogen levels in spaces we occupy could take out a small army. I realize that this kind of group is not for everyone, and there are other ways to make connections. Some women have come and stayed, others have moved away for work, life, and love. Still others have sniffed around a little and moved on, not finding what they needed or not arriving at the right time.

Making connections with others isn't always easy. We are thrown together with peers at an early age and that continues through school. We are then on our own to find people we like and who like us, people we connect with. Sometimes even now when I am making a new friend I feel like I am eight years old again. I am hoping I will get invited to the "cool girls" slumber party because they want to invite me, not because their mom is making them.

There is risk involved with opening up yourself to reveal fears and vulnerabilities, to connecting at our sources of truth. Terry Tempest Williams writes when talking about the idea of exposing our true selves that "we commit our vulnerabilities not to fear but to courage. . . ." Find or re-discover powerful connections in your life. Find a safe place to ask questions and test emerging emotions and fears. It is thoroughly reassuring to speak your truth and see heads bob in understanding of what you are saying. The words, "I know just what you mean. I feel the same way," will liberate you when they are said to you. Make time in your life and space in your heart for connecting with others. Embrace it wholly with the most terrified, tentative parts of your spirit. The rewards are limitless, the power immense.

WHO LOVES YOU, BABY?

Your women friends do. So why not find a way to get together as women? *For Goddess' Sake* guides you in gathering a group of gals to dine with, laugh with, cry with, and just be with. This is the key to joyful and passionate living: *Be who you are.* You are perfect, no apologies necessary. We do not have to live as we have been told. We must live as we desire. And most important, we are allowed to change our minds as often as we feel the urge to.

For Goddess' Sake encourages and provides guidelines for cre-

Good Boys and Bad Boys

We confuse the heck out of men by telling them to be sensitive, but not too sensitive. What does that mean? A man I know was telling me he and his friends were perplexed: Did women want them to be kind and considerate or dangerous and ride a Harley? What do we want? I agree with him. It must be very confusing for men these days.

Here's my theory. It is in our DNA and all our training from day one to try and attract a mate. We are hard-wired for it. We want to be chosen. We want them to choose us. So, when they do choose us and they are kind and considerate, we can't help but hear our little primal voices saying, "Now you have him, but look over there; you don't have that one. He hasn't picked you yet, better get busy." We love the thrill of the chase as much as men do. And we all want to be the one, even for a brief shining moment.

ating a monthly gathering space and place for women to eat, drink, be merry or blue, ecstatic or still—to come together to participate energetically if not vocally, offering their individual dynamism. Listening and allowing is a lovely intention. Put the business connections and networking notions aside and focus on meeting regularly to just *be*.

We will meet twelve goddesses from legends and myths a bit farther on in the book. Most will probably be familiar to you, but they haven't been introduced to you like this before. I offer their intriguing aspects and their powerful, emphatic traits that make them mythic role models and mighty archetypes. From proud and sexy Aphrodite to sanguine Earth mother Hestia to independent, feisty Lilith, all twelve glory girls will inspire and encourage you to love the life you live and be the Great Goddess of your own realm.

BADGES? WE DON'T NEED NO STINKIN' BADGES!

Sure you do. Who doesn't want to earn their gold stars? C'mon. Don't you remember in grade school getting your assignments back with stars or animal stickers on them? What a thrill! We aren't rewarded often enough for brave deeds or for good work when we grow up. We are never too old, too mature, or too anything to love the thrill of applause, just desserts, or a pat on the back. And I am not talking about rescuing-someone-from-drowning kind of brave deeds. I am talking about your own individual courageous steps and changes, no matter how large or how small. Right now is your chance to earn your goddess badges for personal bravery, new perspective, and trying new things on for size. For each solo task you complete, you will earn a goddess badge. Merit badges for daily acts of spiritual discovery and emotional courage, if you will. I am not talking about saving the world. I am a big fan of small steps triggering huge life leaps. And we love prizes. Accomplish the task, earn your badge. Win all twelve, and you are well on your way to new self-awareness and understanding. That can only lead to joy in my mind.

BUT WAIT—THERE'S MORE!

The activities and projects described in each goddess section are designed to ignite new emotions, thoughts, and dreams, or to reassure you of what you may already know. The group celebrations will help create a warm and supportive environment in your gal pal gatherings to explore your similarities, differences, and questions. I share lots of stories from my own experience with my goddess group. And I'm still not done with you yet!

How about a food distraction? *For Goddess' Sake* offers you recipes for delicious dishes and treats and luscious concoctions for your body. Everyone gets fed and pampered in this book, just the way it should be. Some of the recipes in the book have stories of their origin attached, and some are tried-and-true con-coctions from my goddess group get-togethers.

Each meal shared together can evoke a theme through the food or the discussion. The aim is to focus for that bit of time on the feelings, emotions, or information the group or individuals want to bring out. See where discussion and emotions lead you.

Oh, and there are plenty of dog tales in here, too. And a recipe for healthy delights for your best canine pal. Dogs make sense to me, and they tell great stories. Several goddesses—Hecate and Artemis, among others—are always associated with their trusty hounds. I guess I am one of them, too. Ahh, dogs and their women. It is a beautiful thing. Sorry to the cat people out there, I know how you love your felines. I am just more familiar with canines.

THE GODDESS POLLYANNA

Okay, so I was designed to be positive. . . . The glass isn't just half-full; it is always overflowing. I won't apologize, but I wanted this to be the one disclaimer at the beginning. *For Goddess' Sake* is not a scholarly work, although plenty of exploration and dis-covery was involved. I've put a good spin on all the goddess tales and myths I offer. I am a big fan of the goddess Pollyanna, by the way. What can I tell you?

There is always an upside or a flicker of light to be found. I like to see the good where I can. I have chosen to focus on the positive and empowering aspects of each goddess' story. And again, aspects that were previously thought of as negative are not presented as negative here. We can interpret adjectives any-way we want to. Not all the different interpretations of the goddesses' stories are included, but I never set out to write an encyclopedia. So don't send letters asking me why I didn't include so-and-so and why weren't there any Norse goddesses highlighted or telling me that there is no proof that Lilith actually existed according to ancient tablets found in a gas station in Bethlehem.

Here you have my versions of the stories of goddesses that spoke to me. Their messages, lessons, or strengths seemed inspirational and good ones to pass along to you. There are hundreds of goddesses to explore, from many different cultures and

Chain, Chain, Chain

Don't you find those e-mail chain letters that threaten you with bad luck for decades if you don't pass them along to at least twenty-five people within thirty seconds of receiving them just the most upsetting and imposing things ever? Don't send them. Don't threaten your friends with plagues and pestilence. It just isn't very thoughtful.

religions. I am sure every woman would choose differently, but I hope that some of these high-test gals will speak to you, call to you, inspire you, maybe for the first time. There are many good books and resources out there that can add to what I offer; I leave it up to you to search out others on your own. Hopefully, there are women and men in your life who have encouraged you or women that have come before you and whom you respect also. You will likely recognize aspects of yourself and others in the stories of the goddesses or identify pieces you may want to bring forth or nurture within.

Some of the goddesses and their stories may trip the guide-wires in your consciousness and some may not—it will depend on where you are in life, your background, your own stories, and how you move through your existence. Yes, there are light and shadow sides, but the information here does not come with warnings about what happens if you cross the Goddess Sekhmet or don't honor Isis in the prescribed way. There are no threats of bad news—that's not how this works.

Goddesses are not wrathful either, in my book, and it is my book, so there you have it. Approach this and them with an playful heart and mind. This book is a reminder about all that is possible and all things possible. Life is here to participate in, to savor, to taste, and to roll around in, to somersault through. Read on. We have a lot to cover!

GATHERING THE GALS

There are two ways of spreading light: to be the candle or the mirror that reflects it.
—Edith Wharton

The energy of women gathered is extraordinary—healing, exhilarating, sometimes over the top, but always inspiring. Women have been gathering for centuries for friendship, strength, and solidarity. Women's circles have existed throughout time, and we have joined together during our cycles in moon lodges and red tents across many cultures and throughout the world. This time together, away from men and everyday obligations, is a chance for communication and understanding. Celebrations are born and rites of passage noted and observed as a result. Sacred time and space is created with these gatherings, a place to find solace, joy, and commonality. It can be empowering and enlightening to spend time with other women on a regular basis.

MY GALS

My goddess gals, they are a grand bunch. We have laughed until we fell over, sang at the tops of our lungs, greeted the sun with yoga, traveled to the sea and to the woods, and eaten some of the most delicious meals together. The food always tastes luscious when we are together, no matter what. If we order takeout and drink beer it is a banquet. The joy of working together to create meals can be magically tranquil and energizing. For some gals, cooking is stressful, so that needs to be respected. For a few of us, cooking is grounding and the kitchen our place of peace and empowerment. We always balance out our cooking groups among kitchen goddesses and those who are happy to be choppers, stirrers, and servers—works like a charm; like butter, in fact.

The happy hum of the gals in the kitchen buzzing around and doing their own thing is especially joyful. I can freeze-frame moments from our cooking escapades and sigh at the memory of the contentment and simplicity of those times together. All of our special goddess spice added to the meals makes for a sure-fire feast. Simple understanding and acceptance creates an atmosphere for the delicious to settle on every tongue. So read on and learn how to gather together a group of goddesses on your own. Laughter and a little mischief awaits, with many added treats here and there.

SHE STARTED IT

Let me tell you about my goddess group and how it evolved. Nine-ish years ago Heather was the new gal in town from California. Her husband was going to graduate school here in Boston, and she was looking to meet people and make some friends while she was on the east coast for a few years. A woman she knew back home had a sister in Boston. The sister in Boston had a friend who was an art director at an ad agency. The friend at the ad agency had a friend from the town they both used to live in. And the friend from the ad agency had just met a woman who was representing a photographer—and so the first goddess dinner convened at a campus apartment over wine and pizza. It happened that easily. We get together once a month for dinner, sometimes at restaurants but usually at some-one's house for a more intimate atmosphere, or just in case we all get to laughing very loudly (and you just know that someone is going to snort or choke or spew wine across the table in the process), telling bawdy tales, or needing to have a little cry. It offered a chance to just be women for an evening. We are still mothers, daughters, partners, businesswomen, but in this company we are free to speak our fears, hopes, and dreams without having to explain ourselves or play just one role.

Nearly a decade later, some of the characters are the same and some have changed. Heather is happily ensconced back in sunny California but keeps in touch and encourages visitors. She even started a west coast branch. We have recently become international, with a Goddess-UK chapter created by one of our lovely original members up and running.

THE WHYS AND WHEREFORES

My top five reasons to create, join, or belong to a women's group are:

5. It gets you out of the house and out of your head.
4. It provides a dream sanctuary.
3. It gives you a place to listen and be heard.
2. You get to just be.
1. It makes you feel good!

5. *Gets You Out of the House and Out of Your Head.* Having something to look forward to on a day or a week that may be feeling pretty gray otherwise can shift everything to the positive

side. It sets in motion assured and joyful anticipation. We can get into routines that can lead to ruts if we aren't aware of it. Attending a get-together will cause an energy shift in us no matter what. Instead of being alone with too many thoughts and a bowl of cereal for dinner, or with our families or partners and not an inch to ourselves, for a few hours we can get away from it all. There may be times when you are busy or tired and think about not attending. I can tell you that those are the days and nights you will be happiest you got yourself there.

We can revel in our sisters' hopes, dreams, and concerns, generate food and drink and laughter. Sharing a good laugh is an automatic energy and mood lifter. It shakes us out of our own way for even a little bit of time. Laughter is bonding and liberating in the company of women. Not to mention that there's safety in numbers. It is great to have a posse, to know that no matter what, your gals will back you up. Even and especially when you have talked yourself into believing a course of action is a good one for you, your posse will find a gentle way to remind you that you may want to rethink it. I love to know the girls are on my side no matter what.

4. *Provides a Dream Sanctuary.* We all have dreams. Every single one of us. They may change weekly or daily or even hourly. There may also be sneaky, squeaky dreams that have hung in

there for a long, long time, looking for the chance for some air-time. In the company of other women is the perfect place to reveal dreams large and small, old and new. These gatherings offer dream sanctuary, a place to be nurtured and supported. Just because you say the dream out loud does not mean that you have to follow through with it the next day or ever. You may be inspired to take a step, and if you do will have a built-in cheering section. You can ask for help with emotional support or with practical and specific advocacy. Some groups exist to do just that. Dreams are vocalized, and the whole team figures out the steps and make the plans to help make it happen, supporting the dreamer at every step of the way. Gatherings are a wonderful place to whisper or shout your dreams into being, or to just let them hover in the air like fairy dust.

3. *Gives You a Place to Listen and Be Heard.* To have the opportunity to speak and be heard is so powerful. We may have chances to be listened to in our daily lives, but how often are we really heard? Heads nodding in understanding when we speak is a mighty cue to well-being, especially if we aren't used to it. Here is the chance. Knowing that you will be heard and still loved and appreciated no matter what you say is a significant part of gathering together. You may also learn to listen. As women, we have a tendency (here is my generalization of the

moment) to want to jump in and make everything better, often before someone has even finished telling her tale. (There, I said it. If this doesn't apply to you, then I apologize.) Listening to other women speak gives us a turn at understanding what they may be asking for. Maybe they don't want their comment of insecurity refuted. There are times when we just need the opportunity to say, "This is how I am feeling right now and I just had to say it out loud." Wow, does that ever feel good. There isn't anything to fix or make better, no response necessary.

I get chills every time I have the opportunity to speak my truth at the moment or to witness another women speak hers. It takes some practice to become a better listener, and the group will offer you a perfect place to rehearse. Learning how to let questions that haven't even been asked lie still without a response is a valuable practice.

2. *You Get to Just Be.* We run around all day playing a thousand different roles. We are moms to some, and at times not just to our offspring. You know what I mean, caretaker girls. We are partners in love and or business. We are most often the managers of the household. We are the good daughters and the vulnerable little girls. We are bitchy when we need to be and sometimes just because. I tell you, those plates on sticks are spinning pretty fast most of the time, and it takes a lot of effort

to keep them all going. Gathering with other women offers a place to be women in all of our glorious crazy-quilted selves. We understand our moods, or at least recognize them, and don't need explanations or justifications. Of course, we bring all of ourselves with us when we gather, and that is the expectation. Being in the company of other women offers breathing room and the space to sigh. Isn't that a lovely respite from the noise and expectations of the outside world?

1. *It Makes You Feel Good.* The most straightforward benefit of forming a women's group is that it makes you feel good. It may not get any simpler than that, and what a great motivation. If the prospect of getting together with other women makes you happy, then we are just getting started. Don't you love it when you run into a gal pal you haven't seen in awhile, or a woman you may have met once or twice and feel connected to, and out of one of your mouths pops, "Have you had lunch yet?" or "Do you want to grab a cup of coffee?" Gathering regularly with a group of gals gives you that and then some. I am thrilled every time I connect to someone new, and it's such a natural to find a cozy café or park or someone's kitchen to make it happen. Imagine the good feelings that emerge when you have a regular time scheduled to meet with other women. It's something to count on and to look forward to.

DID I JUST SAY THAT OUT LOUD?

The intention of gathering with a group of women is not for therapy, but it may indeed be therapeutic in ways you never imagined. This gathering is also different from a business or networking group. Connections and referrals may be created organically once you get to know one another and trust is established, but this is time to make a spectacle of yourself if you want, to be whoever you want, not to necessarily be on your best behavior. You are not trying to impress potential clients, bosses, or employees.

Women are naturally supportive because that is what we do. Just be aware of the tone you want to set for the group. There is great benefit from gathering over a common theme or interest like a book group, investment club, or workout get-together, but it doesn't always give you the chance to talk off-topic for any length of time. Think about asking one or two women from a group you are already a part of or affiliated with to your goddess group. Go with the gals that have lovely, in-your-face good energy or are quietly intriguing, and mix it up to see what happens.

Let's be clear though. I do not advocate women's groups as a place to condemn men (or women for that matter). It is inevitable that challenges in relationships will become topics of conversation, but this is a place of dialogue and understanding, not a place to foster misunderstanding and bad feelings.

HOW TO START YOUR OWN GODDESS GROUP

What do you want to do? What has the little voice inside been asking for, dreaming of? Now would be a perfect time to listen, join together with other women to support each other's choices. I am hoping that *For Goddess' Sake* will inspire you to conspire with cohorts and shout out your dormant dreams and create a safe and lively place to put those fantasies on their feet. Here are some suggestions for doing just that.

Not Another Mary Tyler Moore Party

Use your instincts when putting your group together. Follow your hunches about mixing and matching gals. They may not always be what you were thinking they would be, but it is a good place to start. Do you remember watching the *Mary Tyler Moore* show in the '70s? Come on, you remember: throwing the hat in the air, the newsroom? Poor Mary would always try to put together a party, and everyone she invited had some kind of funky energy that kept the party simmering down in the doldrums. Rhoda would bring some loser guy or meet some loser guy there, Mr. Grant would be crabby and critical, Murray would try to be supportive with one-liners, Phyllis would hit on Mary's date, and Ted would just be Ted, annoying and needy. I was weaned on television, so you will have to indulge my pop culture references here and there. This is going somewhere, I promise.

We've all been to or had Mary Tyler Moore parties, where something about the mix of people or our expectations or the nervous energy sends the whole atmosphere crashing like out-of-control falling barometric pressure. That's what we are trying to avoid here, so you have to use your instincts and good judgment when putting evenings and women together. A few women you know from the gym, other moms from your children's school, women at work—the gathering does not have to consist of all your best friends. A common connection is a good place to start. Or just someone you've met a few times

True Confession

I want to write steamy historical fiction. I may do it under a pseudonym. I will be using an entirely different voice from the one used in this book. That's very exciting. I can't wait to see how that kind of writing will get activated. Besides asking Aphrodite for a few tips, I may have to try eating different food or listening to music I was never drawn to before or maybe even travel back to Italy or search for Avalon. Who knows, but it will be an adventure.

who seems like a fit. Others can be added as the mood suits. Sometimes you will just get a feeling about including someone or not; they may not be someone you know very well. It will get sorted out pretty quickly, no matter what.

I am chagrined to say that it took me quite awhile to invite one of my dearest friends into the goddess group. It wasn't because I didn't adore her. I think I had to see what the group was going to be for *me*. I knew no one when I joined, so I was really starting with a clean slate as to who I was going to be. Creating a women's group is your chance to do just that. You may not want to include your closest friends at the beginning. We adore our girlfriends, couldn't live without them, but ask yourself first what you are looking for from the goddess group. Invite a few women you have known for a little or a long while and see where it goes. Be sensitive to your instincts about adding women to the group. It doesn't have to happen overnight.

Try not to get too goal oriented with your goddess group. The key, the most basic and only reason to do it, is that it brings you joy. Don't do it under any other circumstances. Each person may have a different idea of how it is going to go or how she needs it to go, and she may not even be aware of it. Even if the first go-around doesn't hold together, it is a process that needs a little nurturing but also some space and time. More than likely, it can work if you get out of the way and allow it to happen. Don't over-think it.

Same Batgirl Time . . .

So, what is this going to look like? Will you meet once or twice a month or every other? What is realistic given people's lives and situations? Maybe you will decide to meet on the first Tuesday of every month or every other Sunday afternoon. Keep it simple—a nice mix of people open to the idea will set the stage. Groups are shaped over time, and if each gal brings in another right away, it may not be a fit. You don't have to all start out as friends; some of you may appreciate your time together but leave it at that. Let it evolve. Women may drift in and drift out again. Timing is a key in everyone's life, and that will change too. Not all women are used to being in groups of women. Not all women have women friends or know how to be one. This isn't an automatic. There will be adjustments here and there. Some women are more comfortable in the company of men. Some women may be more assertive, some more shy. Each of us is on a journey, and we may be able to stay and participate for a little or maybe a long while. We have to give each other the space to discover the answers on our own.

Getting together once a month or so gives you the space to just be a woman—a place where the only expectation is that you show up when you can (and there will be times that you can't either logistically or emotionally, and that is just the way it is— a good group will understand and honor that).

We say we are too busy. We are trying to balance too many identities—partner, wife, mother, teacher, CEO, organizer, employee, daughter, sister, grandmother. We don't make our inner selves a priority often enough. If we stop to focus on the nurturing of our bodies and spirits we can feed ourselves powerful, loving energy. Food can be the conduit, charged with the essence of our true spirits.

Coming Together Over Food

Sitting down to a meal with your beautiful gaggle of gals is a glorious way to exchange energy. It feeds our bodies and our souls, both of which need a great deal of nourishment. Color and taste and smell and emotion all in one bundle, that's what's in store for you when women gather. Rarely in our lives do we allow ourselves the chance to experience just being women; the chance to come together without titles and with only expectations to share good company, eat luscious food, listen, contribute with words or with silent energy. So, here is the chance, and it is well worth setting aside the time for.

Coming together to share food and ourselves creates sacred space. We can close ourselves off from the noise of our lives for a few moments to savor the tastes and textures of a simple or elaborate feast and renew our spirits. We are opening windows and root cellars—where our spirits hide. They want an invitation to dance. They are waiting for the chance to be invited out to play. What a perfect forum. Make the uproar of your everyday become distant background noise or white noise—it isn't going to go away, but it can fade to near-silence for a bit of time. Let the singing of your spirits captivate the space in your bodies and souls that trigger joy and abundance. First you have to invite your spirits to dance, and then the mayhem and merriment will begin. You will be surprised by the feelings and emotions released when you connect with your spirit, opening doors, filling spaces neglected or overlooked.

Create a monthly ritual of inviting the chosen friends or acquaintances over for the soul purpose of breaking bread and just being women. That is the lure, and once you get everyone together, a great energy exchange is born. Food nourishes our bodies and our souls as we transform the energy into joy as we are consuming it—joy of the company, joy of the exchange, joy of the deliciousness.

Yada Yada Yada

Talk, laugh, eat, and drink. It is pretty straightforward and easy to follow. Each meal together can evoke a theme through the food or the discussion. (Wait until you see what's in store for you in the chapter 3—the goddess chapter. Let the games begin!) Or you can simply come together and eat; all will be revealed as the time goes on. The aim will be to focus for that bit of time on the feelings, emotions, or information that the group or individuals want to bring out. See where discussion and emotions lead you. It can be free flowing, and conversations will evolve. You can choose a topic for conversation beforehand if you like. It always makes for a high-energy evening. In my group we have talked about being and having parents, having versus not having children, sex—when, where, how we like it or not, among others. As our lives progress and we add experiences, it is likely that topics will come up quite naturally. When the group has been meeting for awhile, there will be chances to bring up questions about life, love, and death that may have been burning a hole in your eager mind for years. What a lovely environment to let yourself be heard in.

Coming together provides access to delight, inspiration, and remembering that we are complex ageless and timeless beings. When we face passages in our lives, we bring all of ourselves with us, from before we were born up to this very minute. We don't transform into a new being without being influenced by all of our experiences and emotions, wants and desires. Our transition through menopause, for instance, certainly involves physical, emotional, and spiritual changes. We tend to focus on the physical, sweep under the rug, write off, or medicate the emotional, and never even address the spiritual shifts that are occurring. But we are our most powerful beings at this stage of our lives. Our energy is squarely focused on ourselves, a shift from attention to and nurturing of others. This may be a challenging adjustment because we aren't used to being the focal point. Our concentrated alchemy holds pure power and inspiration for us if we recognize it. It can be a time of freedom and confidence, knowing and pride.

Hey, Beauty!

Why does the advertising world decide that we should all want to look like models? Because it is unattainable but we will buy lots of their products in hopes of getting anywhere close; but you knew that already, right? Are you all riled up? Good. Go teach your daughter, niece, or neighbor how to be a conscious consumer and to love who she is right this minute, just that way she is. And I'm not saying throw the products away. It feels great to feel beautiful. I know, I know it does. I just wish we could find more ways from within more often than from without. You really are more beautiful when you feel it on the inside. Did I digress again? Sorry, just so much to talk about.

We can choose any path with our trunks packed full of knowledge, emotion, and strength in the most grounded and celebratory way. All roads have led us right here, right now. Forget regret—waste of time and energy. Here you are, so what are you going to do about it? Use now to be present and thankful for beautiful you and for the extraordinary *compadres* who share the ride. Go on and climb into your T-bird convertible, tie a scarf around your head, grab your sexiest sunglasses, and step on the gas, girlies. These are the divine moments in the company of female spirit, kinship, and grace. They are seasons to be savored.

Taking a Break

My best friend from third to sixth grade was Catherine. We were pretty much inseparable. We sat next to each other in class and rode our bikes around the neighborhood or hung out at each other's houses watching *Dark Shadows* and listening to Sly and the Family Stone or the Beatles after school. There was a brief period, that felt like years of course, when we weren't speaking to one another. It was some girl miscommunication event that got blown up into the biggest thing in life. I doubt either one of us ever really knew what it was about. One day the feud was over, just like that, and we fell right back in step. Maybe it was just a way to take a break from each other.

Gal pal friendships can be so intense, sometimes it can be overwhelming. Keep that in mind down the road if feelings like that come up. You might just have to take a little break. It is a great topic for discussion by the way, one of those, "I know how you feel" kind of subjects.

Solitude should never be underestimated in its ability to regenerate and boost our spirits. There may be periods of time when you feel too exposed or vulnerable to be part of a group. Your greater desire may be to hibernate on your own. Honor these moments or months.

Go Away

As the group gels and stabilizes, you may want to venture out, spend more time together, like a weekend or longer. Weekend retreats are guaranteed to renew your spirit. Take off together as a group to the woods, the desert, or the sea for a longer bit of time, create cooking groups to prepare meals, and plan outdoor activities—yoga, walks or hikes in silence, moving meditations, drumming, primal screams, or songs. Build a labyrinth and then walk it as a group or individually. The added time together and away from your everyday is restorative. Everything does not have to be a group activity—flexibility and options are a must. Solo time is essential for most.

Eve-olution

Let your group evolve. The feeling and flavor will emerge. Whatever works—some things will and some things won't. Defining the group and expectations will form over time. You will find each other and create it together. Instead of establishing rules right away or ever, take some time to clarify the intention of the group. Personality clashes and control issues may appear, but if the intention is agreed upon, you have a clear place to begin from. I am not a big fan of rules, but a general understanding and clarity of where you are starting from are good to discuss. One group I know of meets virtually in a chat room on the Internet. Four of them met at a dude ranch one summer and hit it off. The only problem was they lived all over the country, so getting together was challenging. They log on at the same time once a month to chat and catch up.

I love keeping in touch with my friends far away that way, too, but there is nothing like being there in person. That is something that cannot be reproduced electronically. The rush of the group gathered together is palpable like being under a down comforter on a stormy night or the feeling in the theatre before the curtain goes up. The energy is sparkly and alive and absolutely infectious.

Supermodel Shootout

Groups aren't for everyone, and no two groups will ever be the same. Your goddess group may be sparked in an instant with a perfect mix of energy and personalities, but more likely it will take some time to shape. Expect growing pains and roll with them. Maybe you get together once a month and maybe more or less. It will evolve and sort itself out. What you do when you gather is another story altogether.

My friend told me about a women's group that gathers in the woods once a year with lots of good food, wine, life-sized photos of supermodels, and rifles. You can probably imagine where this is going. One of the weekend activities is to use the photos as target practice. It may not be how I choose to spend a weekend, but something about the sight of those babes sipping wine with rifles on their laps waiting to reload for another round just cracks me up. It brings to mind that great statistic that says there are only a handful of supermodels in the world and the rest of us 60 billion women really don't look like that. Nothing personal to you who do look like that, you're just an easy lot to target because most of us don't. I know it doesn't mean life is automatically easy and wonderful either when you are thought of as falling-down gorgeous. We all have our stuff. No one gets a pass. We are all beautiful, let's help remind ourselves and each other on a regular basis.

Open the door wide, get out of the way, and let in any wandering goddesses in the shape of moods, inspirations, and passions. You can always send them home if they get too unruly, and invite them back on another day.

PEP TALK

"There is no use trying," said Alice; *"one can't believe impossible things." "I dare say you haven't had much practice,"* said the Queen. *"When I was your age, I always did it for half an hour a day. Why, sometimes I've believed as many as six impossible things before breakfast."*
—*Lewis Carroll,* Alice Through the Looking Glass

Forming a women's group is a part of your spiritual practice. And your spiritual practice is a voyage of discovery; it is always changing and always in flux, always in motion. It will vary depending on where your attention is turned to and what is taking up all your time and energy, and on what you discover along the way. So, what jazzes you? What have you learned about you? What do you and don't you believe? What have you picked up on your way to the ball and what have you left behind in the recycling bin on the curb? We are always changing and changed, with every encounter and every experience, whether we wade tentatively into it or charge toward it with lights and sirens blaring.

How you choose to participate in a women's group is as always, up to you. It is likely to be fluid and everchanging. Your presence will change the energy in the gathering no matter what.

TOSS THE TRAINING WHEELS

Are you waiting for life to fall into place before you are happy or find joy in the everyday or like yourself even the littlest bit? There's nothing to practice, and no reason to wait. You are here at this moment, to make it whatever you want most deeply in your heart. You really don't need the training wheels any more, so toss them. Fling them into the trash and start pedaling. This, life right now, is what has been waiting for you, not the other way around.

LIFE AS A PASSIONFRUIT

I eavesdrop. I admit it. I am so often inspired by conversations, whims, and passions floating around out there and wandering by. I love listening to how people interact; their tone, the inside jokes, the hushed notes, and sometimes the outburst of giggles. Don't you love that moment when you get let in on the gag or are allowed into the moment? Someone makes eye contact with you as they are laughing, notices you, and smiles?

One day, standing in line at the grocery store, I was struck by the ease and playfulness of the two women's conversation in front of me. They had to be sisters or great long-time gal pals. One of the women picked up something her friend had put on the belt and said, "Honey, this ugly old thing is way past its goodness date. What was it supposed to be anyway?" She saw me smiling and held it up and said, "I mean look at this thing!" I laughed and shrugged. Her friend jumped right in with, "That's a passionfruit. And it may look funny but you open it up and you will taste life itself, like nothing you ever dreamed of. I just know it comes from paradise."

Open up, girls, and welcome life, direct from paradise. Some days it may seem a bit scruffy, but you don't have to peel away much to discover simple beauty and joy. That is living like a goddess—being open and receptive to the possibility of falling into rapture in every interaction, every encounter, every moment. We are ageless and timeless. We are complex and layered. We are goddesses. We may have been told that as humans we only use a speck of our brain capacity over a lifetime, but more important, we only allow a fraction of our layers to shine through. We are women, but that seems to get overshadowed by our roles as daughters and mothers and lovers and caretakers and partners and high-wire artists—keeping it all in balance. Gather with other women and revel in each other's energy and light. Sparks will fly, and support and understanding will appear like a safety net under that high wire.

I'LL MEET YOU THERE

My friend Jenn lives in a charming old neighborhood in the city. One of Jenn's neighbors is an eighty-two-year-old gentleman named Sam. Sam had been a farmer in the South and was especially interested in Jenn's gardening techniques; he had some expertise in the area and certainly wasn't shy with advice. One spring afternoon Jenn had a question about a plant that had appeared in her garden and walked down the street to see if Sam might come over and identify the new bloom. Sam consented to head back with Jenn. They lived about half a block away from each other, and Jenn was almost home before she realized that Sam walked much more slowly than her. She turned to see Sam a ways back. "That's okay honey, I'll meet you there," he called out to her.

So, it is okay, honey, I'll meet you there. And so will anyone else you invite into your life. They may show up right now or maybe later if you aren't quite ready. They may take it a little slow. And so might you. That's just fine. Slow down, speed up. We all have our own pace and one's not right or wrong, good or bad. All that matters is that it works for you.

A women's group forms organically and energetically. You get to choose how and when you get involved with the process. There will be surprises around every corner, this much I promise.

THE GODDESSES

*How many cares one loses when one decides not
to be something but to be someone.*
—*Coco Chanel*

RED ROVER, RED ROVER,
SEND _____ RIGHT OVER

Every goddess throughout history and across every culture
has a myth or message associated with her. There are
many different versions and interpretations of the goddesses' stories, depending who has gotten hold of them—
men, women, elders—and what is happening in a given
culture at any given time. We certainly know that religious
beliefs and dominance have rewritten many legends,

sometimes making villains out of everyday folk and putting a new twist on the details.

My versions focus on the strength, savvy, and quiet fire of these amazing women. By identifying with those who have gone before us and left their stories in many interpretations, we can tap into their inspiring messages and find strength, clarity, inspiration, and solace for our own lives. I have included here twelve goddesses, to inspire themes for a year's worth of get-togethers with other women. Jump in anywhere that strikes your fancy, or read through in the order they're presented. They are quite eager to play.

Goddesses are archetypes, and every woman has within her all of these elements of each of the goddesses. You contain within you the wisdom of Athena, the curiosity of Pandora, the physical prowess of Artemis, the independent spirit of Lilith, and on and on. Some may be dormant and others dominant. Depending on the time in your life, you may identify or desire the strength or focus of different ones. It is just a matter of remembering that and calling them forth. Pick up the chisel and set free the beauty within. There is no magic involved, just clarity and focus. And it certainly helps to have other gals nearby to remind you and cheer you on.

Let's meet the gals, shall we?

≈ APHRODITE ≈

THE "IT" GIRL OF ATHENS

The beauty beyond bearing,
On an instant of amaze;
All the goddess flaring
From your gaze. . . .
—William Rose Benet,
"The Ghost of Actaeon"

This glorious gal is all about love's abandon and delicious sensuality, and let's face it, she's a vixen. She loves sex and her lusty self, and I find it so inspiring. She is the all-encompassing love goddess and is not to be trifled with. She has sex when, where, and how she wants to and makes no apologies for her passions or appetites. She revels in her nakedness and in her beauty. My favorite part of the legend tells of Aphrodite making love to her young stud Anchises under the mid-day sun, for all to see, with not a care in the world. She is the goddess of our inner harlot, of the seductress that lives in all women. She searches for situations that will take her to another realm of consciousness and pleasure, near madness, to the edge and back again for more. She flaunts her sexual allure, which is at our very essence.

It can instill irrationality in men, for it may be what they fear in us the most. What they can never control. Love and sex in Aphrodite's realm is not rational or practical, but sublime sensory pleasure.

Desire . . . what a great word. It doesn't always have to mean heaving bosoms, corsets, and romance novel covers, although all that is pretty nice, too. Physical desire is fabulous. So is the desire for a big, beautiful, happy life. *Desire* is a grand word. Let's use it. You gotta believe they are out there, the ones that make your heart sweat and your insides tingle. You gotta believe you are trying to find your way to each other. You gotta believe it will happen. And happen your way. It feels great to call the shots—if that means I am a bitch so be it.

SEX AND A TRUCK

Sometimes they are all a gal needs. A man with a truck is a pretty complete package, especially if he also brings food and leaves at the end of the day or the middle of the night. A hunk in a tool belt to fix your leaky faucet, haul your trash to the dump (which is only open on Saturdays from ten to one), pick up a couple of iced coffees and some great pastries, and service you for the rest of the day? Doesn't get much better than that. You get to watch from the doorway as he (or she, hey, it's your

True Oasis

He told me he wanted to show me something magical but that it might take a while to find it. We were hiking in from a small road and there was no trail. The sky was the sharp blue that almost doesn't seem real, the high desert stretched out forever, the hills dotted with scrubby piñon and sage. I said I didn't mind, not a bit. We walked in silence and scrambled up over some craggy rocks. The sun was high and burning, the terrain dusty and uneven. We drank water and laughed and rested and then pushed on. He helped me over one last steep part, and suddenly we were at a large grouping of rocks with a pool of water. We walked up and around and were now standing on top of the rocks and looking down on a waterfall. We jumped off the rocks into the water. We splashed and kissed under the waterfall and then climbed back up to the top and lay down to dry in the sun. Our hands touched and we were still, silent.

Later on we hiked back down and came around the corner to a most glorious sight. There reclining on boulders and in the water were half a dozen naked goddesses. No one spoke. We smiled and continued on our way. You never know what you will come across out there in the world, moment to moment. It is beyond imagining. I can find that place inside alone now when I want and need to, that place of warmth and wonder.

fantasy) tosses the bags oh-so-nonchalantly into the back of the truck, gives you a leer, says, "I'll be right back," and means it. Ahhhh, don't you just have goose bumps? I am not talking about finding random strangers and dragging them back to your cave (although . . .).

Aphrodite gives you permission to call up an ex-flame or new crush or object of lust and tell him or her you need help with some household or yard project. You don't have to act utterly helpless when asking, just a simple favor will do. Most men like to be asked for help, I promise. Make sure they bring their own tools so they have plenty of chances to impress you with their prowess. Who knows where it will go, but you will at least get in a great round of flirting. You are on your own for the seduction end of things, but hot, sweaty fooling around . . . well, excuse me, I have to go make a call.

BEAUTIFUL BUDDHA BELLY

I was minding my own business under the turbo hairdryer at the salon the other day and began to browse through the magazines. I sometimes forget to bring my own reading material, the kind that enlightens instead of depresses me. The ubiquitous fashion magazines at salons don't often make me feel too grand. The covers alone are enough to send me into a funk on certain days. You know the days I am talking about. Don't you wish you could walk around with your own personal airbrush artist sometimes? But I digress. I picked up a copy of a popular woman's glam mag and opened it. There was a voluptuous woman lounging on a sofa and the title was, "Princess of Pleasure." Well, that certainly caught my attention. This magnificent woman helps women reclaim or discover their sensuality and identity as sexual lovelies. How wonderful! I dashed a copy to my editor saying, "This is what I am talking about. This is what I am writing about!" She was thrilled, thank goodness.

Isn't it grand when your beloved adores all the parts of you, even the ones that make you wrinkle your nose and wonder how they ended up on your body or as a part of your personality? Like the Buddha belly, the not-too-taut arms, that toe that hooks in, the fur on your arms, the tiny snore that escapes as you are just falling asleep, your know-it-all nature and unwillingness to back down in an argument? When you call upon Aphrodite, she accepts and loves these parts of you, and wants you to as well. It doesn't matter if anyone else does. It only matters that you do, although it sure is nice to hear it from someone else. Remember, Aphrodite was making love to her young stud in the middle of the day for all to see. She wasn't worried what the other folks thought. It was all about her and pleasure. Aphrodite wants you to feel free and to love (or be open to

Juicy Bites

Here is what I wish for you . . . that moment before you bite into a peach or an orange and it tastes like the middle of summer, that sensory experience is already swirling around in your body before you taste it. Can't you just hear it saying, "C'mon take the bite, go ahead. You know it is going to taste like heaven! Let's go, let's go." Juicy and tangy and sweet all at once. Here's what I hope you don't say: "I sure hope it isn't mealy and dry." Doesn't that thought just send you crashing? We know because we have all had mealy bites in life. So cheers to juicy bites in life. Come to expect them. They're right there next to you.

someone else adoring) all the ranges of you. She is the goddess to acquaint you with a devil-may-care attitude about your body and lovemaking and all the delicious sensual pleasures in the world. It isn't just about sex. It is all that we do for our bodies, how we feed them, how we celebrate them.

We aren't just our bodies. Our bodies are just simply the containers for our energy-rented apartments or villas, if you will. We are not our bodies, but we are trained to think that—to see on the surface but not to delve into the spirit strata within. So, when ➤ we tap into the energy of the goddesses, it is not difficult to call it to us—it is there all the time. We just have to access it by inviting it in, remembering to open the door and to keep it open when the guests arrive.

We must love our containers because they house and nurture and protect us. We duct tape the lids on so tightly sometimes that we forget that all the magic is contained within. Contained? Yikes! Did you hear that? We don't need to contain our energy, we need to unleash it and soar and sing and spin around in circles with our heads thrown back until we get dizzy and fall over in a heap of laughter. My year-and-a-half-old nephew was doing that the other day—just spinning around and shaking his head, then stopping and falling over, laughing and laughing—a natural high. Our bodies are our splendid packaging—every soft and squishy or bumpy and bony part. Love what you have right now. It is perfect.

★ Earning Your Aphrodite Badge ★

ON YOUR OWN: SHAMELESS HUSSY

Now, let's be clear about flirting: I have been known to flirt with men, women, children, animals, and house plants if I think I might get a reaction. Sometimes I am very aware that I am doing it, and other times I am oblivious. Okay, I lied. I don't think I am ever completely unaware that I am doing it. It is just so much fun.

Flirting does not mean you want to sleep with someone (not necessarily). It is about connection and sparks and being in the same time, space, and energy field with someone or something. It is electrifying. It is about now, the moment, and the intoxication of possibility.

I often picture the Michelangelo fresco on the ceiling of the Sistine Chapel, the part where the hand of God is reaching out to touch Adam's hand (although somehow in my vision it's always a woman's hand he is reaching toward). That's the kind of connection I am talking about. You've felt it. I know you have. Don't you want more of that? Get out there and flirt. It doesn't have to mean anything more than, "Hey, I see you. Isn't it amazing that we are both here in this very spot on this wildly spinning planet?" Everybody feels good. Give it a try next time you are out and about. Hold your eye contact a minute longer, smile a bit bigger, laugh out loud when someone tells you something funny. Report back to the group at your next get-together. Share your story and earn your badge.

GROUP CELEBRATION

★ ☽ ★

Fantasy Land

You have to give this a try. My gals once created a goddess harem at a weekend gathering. We set up lovely fabric as a tent over the dining area and cooked Mediterranean food. The dining room was lit with many, many candles, and the Middle Eastern music on the stereo capped the mood of enchantment. One of our lovelies had taken belly dancing lessons and changed into her outfit and danced for us all. It was such a joyful evening. We were all transported far away by the energy and color and rhythm of the evening. Of course, we did end up talking about sex that night too, if memory serves.

Create your own women's tent with your group, or build an evening around a place or theme with food, music, and decorations. Grab a beautiful scarf or veil and give belly dancing a try, or drumming and African dance. It is truly tuning into your feminine core and so delightful. Dance before or after supper, and then share your fantasies or tell a really great seduction story. Fantasy time works wonders to get us out of ourselves and our immediate world and into the realm of possibility.

RECIPES FOR APHRODITE

Chocolate-Dipped Fruit

You know the girl needs a little chocolate. Perfect for being fed to by a handsome hunk. And there's not a lot of time or work involved.

> 8 oz. semisweet chocolate
>
> 1 tablespoon butter
>
> 1 cup each of dried mangoes, apricots, and papaya

Melt chocolate and butter in a saucepan over low heat, stirring occasionally. Line a cookie sheet with waxed paper. Dip half of each piece of fruit in the chocolate mixture and place on the cookie sheet. Allow to set for 2 to 3 hours, until firm. Store in refrigerator (in a container for up to three days) if you are distracted by other activities.

Moneypenny's Perfect Martini

This is my friend Craig's recipe. He loves martinis and looks great drinking them. Here's his story to go with it:

No doubt you remember James Bond's penchant for a perfect martini—shaken, not stirred. And as Sherlock Holmes had Mycroft Holmes, so too does 007 have 001, his grandfather, the original James Bond.

Please keep in mind, James's grandfather was in Her Majesty's service when the sun never set on Great Britain's empire. Was the world less complicated? This much we know: Upon Bond's return to his Sussex estate, Moneypenny, he was always greeted by Em, his loyal valet, and his favorite tonic, Moneypenny's Perfect Martini.

$1/4$ cup Cointreau

1 fresh clementine or orange

3 oz. Malacca Gin

$1/2$ oz. extra dry vermouth

2 drops Angostura Bitters

Drizzle Cointreau into a beautiful 4-oz. or larger glass, coating the entire interior. Place glass in the freezer for one hour. Go do something fun or daring and come back later.

Remove glass from freezer. Shave the rind of either a clementine or orange, twist over the glass, releasing the essence, and rub along the rim. Place glass back in freezer while you fill a shaker with lots of ice and add gin, vermouth, and bitters. Shake rhythmically for 30 seconds, imagining a slow waltz.

Remove glass from freezer. Squeeze essence from orange or clementine rind into glass and strain contents of shaker into it. Add rind to glass.

Raise your glass in a toast, sip, and repeat Bond's words: "Christ, Moneypenny, that's good."

≈ ARTEMIS ≈

SHE'S A BRICK . . . HOUSE

To protect what is wild is to protect what is gentle. Perhaps the wildness we fear is the pause between our own heartbeats, the silent space that says we live only by grace. Wilderness lives by this same grace. Wild mercy is in our hands.

—Terry Tempest Williams

Artemis is the adolescent huntress—strong and bold and independent. She is a nurturer of living things and creates as well as destroys. She roams the forests with her pack of dogs, travels with the moon, and needs no one. She is represented by the constellation Ursa Major, the Great Bear. Ursa Major, or the Big Dipper, tells us of each coming season with the tip of its handle pointing in a new direction with the arrival of the cycle. Artemis travels where she wants to and when, unencumbered by expectations or others' influences.

Artemis reminds us of our physical strength and the discovery of that strength on our own—in our own time and in our own way. One woman's two-block walk is another woman's marathon. This is between you and your body. It is empowering to feel mighty and to have a heightened awareness of our bodies, and to realize their strength. To know how they move and bend and to push ourselves just a bit further each time we tackle a physical challenge or launch an exercise campaign. Being strong and physically fit is supremely feminine when we are in touch with our bodies and their power in movement. Discovery of our own strength allows us to uncover another layer of self and our unrestrained, primal capability.

WHY DID THE CHICK CROSS THE ROAD?

Because it was driving rain and wind and the semi-tractor trailer was barreling down the road headed right for her. So she grabbed her bike and ran like mad across the bridge. Here's how it all came about. A few years back I saw a flyer advertising a three-day bike ride in support of a health issue. Perfect timing— I had just gotten a new bike and was really enjoying riding around. I didn't put a basket or a bell on it or cards in the spokes or anything, but I was feeling pretty flush. My last brand-new bike might have been my purple banana-seat number with the big bright flowers when I was twelve, so it had been awhile.

I got very excited about the ride and started raising pledge money from family and friends. I also tried to convince some folks to come with me. I had several "flat out No's" and a few

Dog Is My Co-Pilot

My friend Jane and I are always looking for places to substitute *Dog* for *God*. We don't mean to offend anyone, so sorry if it hits a nerve. It just makes us both smile to picture our dogs in the passenger seat of the car with their ears flapping in the wind. Fairy Dogmother is a favorite. The idea of my old black Lab dressed as a fairy with wings and a wand gets me laughing. I love *Dog bless,* too. I sign books that way if I know it is for a canine fan. There are a lot of good ones. It's fun to turn things upside down and around.

Dog philosophy is very straightforward. Eat, sleep, and experience. Life is full every minute of every day. What's next? Are we going for a ride? Are you going into the next room? Well, I'll come too. Did you hear that? I'll go check it out, don't worry. And I don't think they walk away from an encounter saying, "Can you believe that collar she is wearing? It so clashes with her spots." I am pretty sure that thought never crosses a dog's mind, a bitch's Yes, a dog's, No. We all do it sometimes and that is fine, too. Dog bless us one and all.

"Maybes." A few days before the event I had several people still on the fence about joining me. The night before I checked the weather, and my heart raced a little when I saw that it was supposed to rain for the next three days—not just drizzle, we're talking pouring rain with high winds, a good ol' Nor'easter. I was on my own, all the fence sitters begged off at that point. They tried to talk me out of going, too. Biking in a driving rain for three days, why not? I didn't mind going by myself; I was just hoping that I wouldn't be the absolutely last person to finish. I wasn't in tip-top shape, but I had done a few long rides and loved the idea of challenging myself.

We were to ride an average of sixty miles a day, staying in summer camps for the night along the way. The first day, I fell in with the group that got lost (tough to see those markers in the monsoon)—so lost that we went about twenty miles out of the way and limped into camp just before dark. We were soaked and exhausted but laughing at dinner after hot showers and changing into dry clothes. Several people from the group dropped out the next day, faced with very sore muscles and more rain. I ventured off on my own and chatted with people as we passed each other. I was wet and wasn't going to be dry for awhile, so I may as well keep riding and finding pleasant moments, I figured. People were friendly and supportive, but I rode most of that day by myself. I got a flat tire in the afternoon, and two gentlemen stopped right away to help. I admit that I let them do the whole thing. They got to be knights, and I got to keep my freezing cold hands in my pockets for a while. When we arrived in camp, we were greeted by music and massage therapists. What an amazing sight. I slept like a baby that night. The other great thing about riding that much is that you can and should eat all the time just to be able to keep going—yay, bonus. The sun came out for the last twenty miles of the ride on our final day. I meandered past marshes and the ocean, up a steep hill and then sprinted across the finish line, and I wasn't last. I was tired, but I felt so exhilarated I could have kept riding forever, or at least a few more miles.

We are so much stronger than we know. Truly. Were there times I was miserable and wanted to quit? Many, many. Did I ask myself what in the world I thought I was doing? On more than one occasion. Did I arrive home feeling strong and capable and proud of myself? More than I can say.

I tend to do things in extremes, so you don't have to follow my lead, but any physical challenge is powerful. Only you know what that means or what that looks like for you. We do feel invincible if we push ourselves physically, and it will spill over into other areas of our life—guaranteed. That experience became a standard for me. I remember it when I am faced with a challenge, and often I can push on through when I recall saying "I think I can, I think I can . . ." over and over to myself riding on the rain-soaked roads.

I See You

I was walking down a snowy street the other day wearing the wrong shoes for the weather, carrying hot tea in one hand and papers in the other. I started to slip. In order not to drop everything, I slowly fell sideways into a snow bank. I laughed because it must have looked absurd. A handsome man walked by just at that moment. He hurried over and said, "Nice save," as he offered his hand. "Well, a partial save anyway," I replied, brushing snow from my hair and trying in vain not to blush too deeply. "No, it was really quite graceful and your laugh was the best part," he said with a sly smile. By then I was crimson.

We don't always have to be at our best or have every hair in place. Sometimes we connect with others and are noticed because we are just being real and human and vulnerable and funny. It's okay to laugh at ourselves; in fact it is necessary.

★ Earning Your Artemis Badge ★

ON YOUR OWN: PUSH IT

You know what I am going to tell you—get out there and challenge yourself! Use that glorious body of yours to celebrate your individual strength and beauty. Walk a little faster, run a little further, dance a bit longer. I've said it before, but in case you weren't listening; pushing yourself in one area of your life carries confidence to all of the other realms. It's a guarantee. So, sign up for that yoga or Pilates class and really show up this time. Join the tai chi group in the park on Saturdays, or plan to run your first 5K road race a few months from now. We have to take care of these bodies we've been blessed with. They give us so much. Earn your Artemis badge by reminding yourself that only you and you alone know the depths of your strength. See what you can do. Celebrate your beautiful body. I know you'll feel good.

GROUP CELEBRATION

★) ★

Quiet Time

My gals and I have hiked in silence on several occasions, and it is a powerful experience. Plan an activity in silence—hiking or walking in the woods or a park works well, no matter the season. You will be amazed at the heightened sounds of nature as you walk. Nothing sends the notion of our impact on the land home with more clarity than hearing the crunch of leaves and sticks underfoot or the squeak of new snow. You can also just go somewhere outside and sit in silence together, find your own space to be in nature. Silence can help focus our attention on activities and their effect on our lives. It is amazing what we hear when we focus on listening. It can heighten our awareness of gratitude for the day. Silence also allows us to hear what we have been drowning out with noise. Outdoor activities lend themselves well to the process, as do creative projects. Try not to set a time limit for the silence, but carry on as long as it feels natural. Give yourself enough time to be present. You can talk about your experience afterward or not. It might be nice to simply write in your journal. Carry the silence over into the meal if you are gathering together to eat afterward.

RECIPES FOR ARTEMIS

Great Goddess Salad

Created by moi, this hearty salad blends foods to feed your soul. Earth, sky, and water elements combine to create a masterpiece of good and good-for-you ingredients. I love to make it for myself or a crowd. It meets with my notion that making a salad is free license to fling any combination of foods you adore together in a bowl and throw dressing on it.

The basics are as follows: Baby greens (the Earth and the spring, creativity and new ideas and emotions born) and for the heart, smoked trout (a nod to the water and life itself), blue cheese (for our lady moon—I still like to think she is made of blue cheese), red onion (fragrant reminder of our own power, strength, and beauty), and toasted almonds (Nut, Egyptian Great Sky Goddess). Here are quantities and quick instructions for making this Great Goddess salad.

1 garlic clove, halved (optional)

Salad

Mixed baby greens and herbs, about 2 cups per person

1 medium-sized smoked trout filet torn or cut into pieces

$1/3$ cup crumbled blue cheese or goat cheese

$1/2$ cup red onion, chopped

$1/4$ cup toasted almonds

$^1/_2$ Granny Smith apple, chopped

Salt and pepper to taste

Cucumbers, roasted red peppers, your imagination (optional)

If you'd like, rub a halved clove of garlic on a wooden salad bowl before mixing the ingredients.

In a large wooden salad bowl, combine all salad ingredients. Toss with a simple vinaigrette made with red wine vinegar. Serves 4 to 6.

Feta Cheese Spread

This is a simple and easy recipe, perfect to make or bring over as an appetizer when you gather.

$^1/_4$ cup finely chopped fresh mint

2 or 3 garlic cloves

4 Tablespoons extra-virgin olive oil, or more

$^1/_2$ Tablespoon fresh ground pepper

8 oz. feta cheese, rinsed, drained, and crumbled

1 to 2 Tablespoons fresh lemon juice, strained

Puree mint, garlic, oil, and pepper in a food processor until mixture is like paste. Add feta cheese and pulse until mixture is smooth and creamy. Adjust seasoning with lemon juice and oil, if needed. Makes about 1$^1/_2$ cups. Serve with toasted pita or vegetables.

≈ CASSANDRA ≈

KITTY CARLISLE OF TROY

If the all too obvious and the overly straight sprouts of Truth and Goodness have been crushed, cut down, or not permitted to grow, then perhaps the whimsical, unpredictable, and ever-surprising shoots of Beauty will force their way through and soar up to that very spot, thereby fulfilling the task of all three.
—Alexander Solzhenitsyn—Nobel Prize
acceptance speech

Kitty Carlisle was one of the gals on that television show *To Tell the Truth*. She always looked fabulous with her coifed black hair, pearls, and quiet presence. Meanwhile, back to Cassandra . . .

Cassandra was a Trojan princess who was able to see the future, but no one believed her. Cassandra was taken prisoner by King Agamemnon after the fall of Troy. Not happy about that, she cursed him and foresaw his death. No one believed her. Agamemnon was in turn slain by his wife Clytemnestra and her new lover, Aegisthus. She told you so. It is usually a good idea to believe a cranky princess; they tend to know what they are talking about. From Cassandra we remember the power of our own truth, not anyone else's, but our own. Listen to your intuition, the gentle or insistent dreams that reappear. They are speaking your truth and guiding you toward new understanding and experiences.

DRAMA QUEEN

I circled the Actor's Studio for three years before crossing the threshold. I had read the flyer advertising acting classes many, many times, but I had never even called Marc, the instructor, to ask him for more details. I kept meaning to. Then I met a woman at a party on a Monday and she asked, "Do you know about Marc's acting class?" followed by, "I'll meet you there tomorrow night. Of course you are coming." I had run out of excuses not to go, and now I was face to face with the fear with nowhere to hide. I was a month away from my fortieth birthday. It was a matter of facing one of my most night-sweat-inducing terrors and biggest yearnings. I wanted to be on stage. What Leo girl doesn't? We can be such drama queens sometimes. I didn't have time to talk myself out of going. The gauntlet had been thrown. If not now, when? I walked through the door the very next evening and was pretty sure I was going to throw up for the first hour. Then I got up on stage. Aha! Cue the angels singing

The Apricot Tree

I planted an apricot pit in a pot of dirt when I was ten. I imagined looking out my grandmother's kitchen window and seeing an apricot tree swaying gently next to the apple trees, hanging around like a little sister. I wasn't sure how long it was going to take to grow, but my grandmother was very encouraging. She promised to keep an eye on the plant for me when I went home to the city. Time passed and I forgot about the apricot tree, but my grandmother didn't. It must have been late in high school sometime when I was visiting and noticed the little tree out the kitchen window. I asked about it and my grandmother said, "Well, that is the apricot you planted back when you were little." That summer ➡

and the trumpets blaring, I was home. The energy that moves through you on stage is extraordinary.

I told someone recently that acting class is the only place where I am not acting. The one place where the truth is revealed automatically. It is the one place where all things are possible, and I am myself as an unrefined and complex offering. What will come up? What will each role trigger or unleash? I can't wait to see what happens. Some nights class is difficult because it offered its first few handfuls of fruit. The tiny apricots were delicate and juicy and delicious. Each year the tree grew bigger and offered more. I loved to tell everyone the story of how I had planted the pit and my grandmother had cared for and coaxed it into a lovely tree. I was the last to realize that this wasn't the same seed I had planted years ago. My mother finally confessed. My grandmother had ordered the tree from a special catalog that sent a species to survive the harsh winters in the Northeast. She really wanted me to believe that it was my tree. That is what grandmothers can do. They make you imagine that anything is possible. Just ask them. They will always tell you it is.

anger or sadness or other challenging emotions emerge. But this is the safe place to let them go, to use them as a creative outlet. I feel them come through the character I am playing and out into the scene, and it is like taking a deep cleansing breath, releasing a trapped bit of stale air. This is the place where we feel it all, where we train to allow all feelings, motivations, and inspirations to flow. All we have to do is let it happen.

This is a life lesson for love and creativity and all that is possible. It is a lovely, challenging teaching in truth and possibility. We all know the truth if we listen to our core and act from there, that place of open flow of wisdom. Marc reminds us so thoroughly and gracefully to jump into the abyss. See what happens. What have you got to lose? Nothing. There is no such thing as getting it wrong or failure in his studio. There is only securely upheld risk taking and wing spreading. The minute you believe that about living your truth in life is a magnificent realization.

The class is a liberating and invigorating experience each week that has carried over into other areas of my life. Not long ago I was invited to an event where I didn't know but one person. I

Sam I Am

I always wanted to be the girl with the long hair who strolled onto the beach at sunset and instantly and effortlessly had people gathered around the bonfire as she played the guitar and sang beautiful sad songs. Now I realize that it was the energy or feeling of the scene that I wanted to create. I don't want to be her, but I want to create that mood, drawing people in and making them feel serene. Maybe it happens with my work. Maybe it happens by who I choose to be out there in my realm. How I interact with people and places I encounter is my creation. How do you want to be in the world?

am usually fairly outgoing, but party situations have become a bit more daunting as I get older. I do love having my posse around, so solo is sometimes intimidating when I am in a mood. As I was walking up to the door I almost turned around to leave. Then I said to myself, "You walked into acting class, you can do anything." In I went and had a lovely time. Acting has become a touchstone for me in so many situations since. Following that curiosity and passion for acting was pursuing one of my truths. I had to wait until I believed this reality myself before I could look any further or take any steps. We lie to ourselves or try to quell the small and large truths brewing and stewing inside us. But why not listen? Why not let those voices be heard and find out what they are asking for and dreaming of? You can be whomever you want to be from day to day or minute to minute.

GROUP CELEBRATION

Poetry and Creative Writing Salon

On one weekend retreat my goddess group did some writing. It was cold and rainy out, and we lit a fire and got blankets and curled up on sofas and in chairs with our pens and journals. Someone threw out a word or phrase and we all wrote for a few

★ Earning Your Cassandra Badge ★

ON YOUR OWN: DREAMSTORMING

Simply speaking your dreams out loud has power and puts that desire into the universe. Don't underestimate it. Make a list of all the things you'd like to try. Is it karate, a whole new career, writing poetry, singing in a band, or jumping out of an airplane?

Ask the group for help shaping a desire you have for your life. Dreams come in all colors and sizes, and it is very likely that you all will be able to support one another in realizing a long-held desire. With your gals is where you will hear, "Of course you can do that, and I have a friend who might be able to help. . . ." Make plans to help your wishes come true. You can create timetables and goals together.

minutes. Sometimes we shared what we had written, sometimes not. We did this for an hour or so and had a nice cozy time. One goddess wrote a beautiful poem about women and the group. Give it a try with your group. Everyone doesn't have to be a writer to have fun. We are all writers and creative spirits. You just never know what might unlock it. Or try reading poetry, scenes from plays, or people's original work—put yourself on the creative line. Take risks in this safe environment. It can be joyful and always inspiring.

RECIPES FOR CASSANDRA

Bring on the Ginger! Cookies

Spicy and bold and with three kinds of ginger, there is no way to ignore the dynamic taste of these treats.

$3/4$ cup unsalted butter, at room temperature

1 cup packed dark brown sugar

$1/4$ cup molasses

1 egg

2 cups unbleached flour

2 teaspoons ground ginger

2 teaspoons baking soda

$1/2$ teaspoon salt

1 1/2 Tablespoons chopped ginger root

1/2 cup finely chopped crystallized ginger

Cream together butter and brown sugar in a large mixing bowl. Beat in molasses and then egg.

Sift flour, ground ginger, baking soda, and salt. Stir into butter mixture with a wooden spoon until blended. Add other gingers and mix well. Refrigerate dough for at least 2 hours or overnight.

Preheat oven to 350°F and grease cookie sheets. Shape the dough into 1-inch balls and place on cookie sheet about 2 inches apart. Bake until browned, about 10 minutes. Remove to racks and cool completely. Makes about 4 dozen.

Squash Risotto

Whenever my goddess gals and I need a little TLC, we make hot yellow and orange delights to feed our second and third chakras. This is one of our favorites for an autumn weekend gathering.

4 Tablespoons unsalted butter

1 large onion, chopped

1 1/2 cups diced, peeled butternut squash

5 cups (or more) chicken or vegetable stock

1 1/2 cups Arborio rice

1 cup dry white wine

$^1/_2$ cup grated Parmesan cheese

$^1/_4$ cup minced fresh parsley

Melt 3 tablespoons butter in large heavy saucepan over medium-low heat. Add onion and sauté until soft and light brown, about 10 minutes. Add squash and $^1/_2$ cup stock. Cover pan and cook just until squash is tender, about 10 minutes. Mix in rice. Add wine and cook until absorbed, stirring occasionally, about 30 minutes. Add $^1/_2$ cup stock and stir until rice is tender and mixture is creamy, adding more stock if too thick, about 5 minutes. Mix in remaining tablespoon of butter and Parmesan cheese. Season with salt and pepper. Divide among bowls and garnish with parsley. Makes 4 to 6 servings, and is easily doubled.

≈ LADY OF THE LAKE ≈

MYSTERY WOMAN

The rest is silence.
　　　　　—Shakespeare, Hamlet *Act 5, scene 2*

Known by several different names and able to take many different forms, this goddess kept everyone guessing and under her
spell. In her mystery she wielded great power. The Lady of the
Lake was the keeper of the sword Excalibur that bestowed upon
Arthur his power as king. She resided on the mystical isle of
Avalon and regained her ancient knowledge from Merlin, whom
she enchanted. Her knowledge and power eventually surpassed
his. She has been known as Viviane and also as Morgan Le Fay
and as a separate entity altogether. Three goddesses were said
to have accompanied Arthur by boat back to Avalon as he lay
dying. Was it three or just one? In the mystery lies her force and
our intrigue. We are not one woman; we are many.

The Lady reminds us that some secrets are sacred. We are
wise not to reveal all of ourselves in haste or without care. We
can be quick to give and give of ourselves until we are depleted
and most weary. Our training is to say Yes to every request
made of us. We offer our hearts so freely and completely that

we can send folks reeling with the depth of energy unleashed in the overture. It can be intoxicating. Sometimes, and not always, but sometimes we may want to explore the landscape a bit before heading out with all our bags jam-packed. A little mystery can be equally as intoxicating. Use it, ladies.

WHEN CARY MET KATHARINE

Cary Grant has a great line to Katharine Hepburn in the movie *The Philadelphia Story.* They are antagonistic exes, and Katharine is about to marry again when Cary gets her involved in an elaborate scheme. She is hardly pleased and tries her best to be furious at him. He responds as only he can, and so seductively, "You are slipping, Red. I used to be afraid of that look. The withering glance of the goddess." Ladies, ladies, ladies, it is our birthright to be mysterious and give withering glances. We can and do baffle men and baffle each other. Practice your withering glance, it is so much fun. Keep people guessing sometimes about what is going on inside. Don't give it all away. We don't have to explain ourselves or justify any of our actions, truly we don't. We are allowed to say "No." We are allowed to sit back and observe instead of jumping in to fill silences and voids. And we don't have to defend our choices or beliefs, ever.

Silent Meditation

Several years ago another goddess lovely and I decided to sign up for a week-long silent meditation in Montana. We would be camping on a ranch and participating in meditations from sunrise to sunset, all in silence. The idea of spending a week with one of my best gal pals and not talking seemed like the biggest challenge of all.

It was a magical time for both of us. Our meditations involved movement, sound, color, stones, and also ranch work. Meals were taken all together, also in silence. We communicated with smiles all week. Lisa and I didn't talk when we were back at the tent; we settled into the peace and simplicity of hearing only the natural sounds around us. At our final dinner we were allowed to talk. Lisa and I both found ourselves wanting to flee back to the quiet of the tent. Talking just felt like noise. The tiny airport the next day seemed like the loudest, busiest place ever. We both agree that many spiritual and emotional shifts occurred for us during that week and continue on several years later. The shared experience made our bond of friendship even stronger. Silencing our minds is truly powerful. So much is released to make room for so much more.

BELLA LUNA

One weekend my goddesses gathered at an old farmhouse. It was the beginning of October in New England, and it was beautiful. Cool nights and days with bright sunshine, mosaics of leaves on the trees and on the ground, and rich blue skies. It would be one of several gatherings at this same house. It became our playhouse in a way, a touchstone of serenity, release, and adventure. We went often enough that all knew the house and the landscape. We each found favorite spots to pause or read or visit. We knew the indoor and outdoor options and settled into our individual and collective whims of our time together. Hikes in the mountains, pilgrimages to the enchanted forest, building a labyrinth in the field, donning funny hats and costumes all became magic memories of our weekends. This weekend took place early on, maybe the second time we had gathered there. Expectation of fall and the changes it brings and the tactile charge of being together sent our enthusiasm and spontaneity soaring.

"Let's go swimming!" one bold goddess put forth in the evening after we had enjoyed a leisurely feast. Shouts of encouragement and random outbursts came in a flurry, and soon there were three of us willing to take the plunge with the moon whispering her sanction from the inky black sky above. Two of us found bathing suits and one other found covering extraneous under such a divine light. Into the pool we jumped and out as quickly we sprang as the icy water shocked us through and through. Our own shrieks and laughter were as loud as the urging shouts from the women at the edge of the water, gathered there with big towels to wrap us in when we emerged. Photos were taken and make us all laugh to this day. I remember the cold, but more often I recall our willingness to partici-pate in a ritual of celebra-tion and audacity, each one of us taking part in our own way to complete the circle, bonding our spirits.

Magic Moments

One morning I sat down at my usual table in my favorite breakfast place and let out a long sigh just as my regular waitress came by. "Oh love, don't do that. Let him come to you. You lose three drops of blood from your heart each time you sigh," she said in her lovely brogue. Must have been written all over my sigh what I was thinking about. Neither one of us said anything more about it.

That brief exchange in the restaurant was one of those magic moments out in the world where someone gives us some-thing new to think about or some new per-spective from their experience. I will never sigh again without remembering. Lovely.

Small moments of daring and camaraderie create everlasting memories of sensation and delight. They never disappear, and they always comfort when we search them out and bring them back in close—always a toasty towel, many hands patting away the cold, and a wink from bella luna. This is why we gather. This is why we make the time and create the memories. This is why we remember.

GROUP CELEBRATION

★) ★

Name That Goddess

Your group can plan gatherings around solstices, new moons, eclipses, or other astrological events. You may also want to have a naming ceremony for the group and for you all as individuals. My goddess gals all have names that have been adopted spontaneously during events or because of character traits, life stories, or special talents. We love having another secret for just us. You will, too. Names will emerge naturally over time, and so you may want to plan a special supper each time a new name is selected or do them all at once at one celebration. Make it special whatever you decide. Your goddess name adds a new dimension to your mystery and power as individuals and as a group.

ON YOUR OWN: A LOVELY BATH

Creating simple rituals can be catalysts for bringing to life hopes and dreams. Transformations and new, clear energy can emerge. Candles can be used for burning written wishes and water for cleansing moods and old fears. In honor of the Lady of the Lake, we will use her domain of water. If you do not have a bathtub, use a large bowl and just put your feet in the warm water. Add your favorite bath salts. Close your eyes. And dream.

Draw a bath with warm water and add any scents that you like. Lemon is often used in rituals for letting go. Lavender is a peaceful, grounding scent. Sandalwood is used in times of transition, and geranium is an all-around feel-good scent. Use any aroma that pleases you—that is most important. For color, choose yellow candles. Yellow is the color of wisdom. It stimulates the nervous system and heightens spiritual awareness. Create a private sanctuary all your own and plan this ritual for when you will be alone. As you settle into the tub, let your mind quiet and allow preoccupations and the to-do list to float away. Notice any visions and thoughts that rise from the warm water. Offer new desires to the universe, and let them swirl around you.

RECIPES FOR LADY OF THE LAKE

Glorious Goddess Scrub

This exfoliating and moisturizing salt scrub is heavenly in the shower, especially in the winter. Be careful, it does make the tub and shower slippery. Experiment with your gals with different scents and combinations.

> 8 cups (approximate) large- or small-grained sea salt or kosher salt
>
> 2 cups sunflower oil, walnut oil, avocado oil, jojoba oil, or rosehip oil or combine two or more of these oils together
>
> $1/2$ cup aloe vera gel
>
> 1 cup dried roses, calendula flowers, or lavender flowers (optional)
>
> 1 to 2 drops essential oils

In a large bowl combine sea salt with any combination of oils until the salt is covered. Stir with wooden spoon. Add aloe vera gel and mix. Add 1 or 2 drops of essential oils of your choice, and stir again. Dried roses, calendula flowers, or lavender flowers can be added. Spoon into jars. Makes enough for about 4 medium-sized jars.

Crème Brûlée

Crème Brûlée has always seemed mysterious to me. It seems simple, yet it is so elegant and sophisticated. A fitting recipe for our Lady. And for a gathering of goddesses on the night of an eclipse.

This recipe is from my dear friend Lisa Martel, chef/owner extraordinaire. She served it at her wonderful restaurant On the Park in Boston.

2 cups heavy cream

$3/4$ cup sugar

$1/2$ vanilla bean

6 egg yolks

6 Tablespoons brown sugar

Raspberries

Blackberries

Preheat oven to 325°F. Combine the cream, sugar, and vanilla bean in a saucepan, bring to a simmer, and turn off heat. Whisk the egg yolks until they turn pale yellow. Slowly add the cream mixture to the eggs while continuing to whisk so that the eggs don't cook. Remove the vanilla bean; split the bean and scrape out the inside of the pod into the egg and cream mixture. Whisk well.

Fill 6 individual ramekins three-quarters of the way up. Place ramekins in water bath and cook at 325°F until custard is set but still creamy, about 40 minutes. Remove from water bath and allow ramekins to cool at room temperature until they are no longer steaming. Chill ramekins in refrigerator.

About 1 hour before serving, preheat broiler. Sprinkle 1 table-spoon brown sugar on top of each ramekin and spread evenly. Place under broiler until sugar caramelizes. Serve with fresh raspberries and blackberries and a good cup of coffee! Serves 6.

≈ ATHENA ≈

MISS SMARTYPANTS

The mother eagle teaches her little ones to fly by making their nest so uncomfortable that they are forced to leave it and commit themselves to the unknown world of air outside. And just so does our God to us.

—Hannah Whitall Smith, American minister and reformer (1832–1922)

Athena is the patron of heroes, a protector and a diplomat. Her strength comes from her wisdom and faith in her knowing. She is a rational rather than emotional thinker. Athena sprang from Zeus's head as a fully formed beautiful woman dressed in golden armor and ready for battle. I just love the visual of that. She was a trusted advisor and strategist in times of war and peace. She moved easily in the world of men. She was also an accomplished domestic goddess, known for her weaving and crafts. From Athena we learn to be our own wise counsel and to offer our wisdom in the honest truth. She offers guidance to our creative selves as well and encourages us to call upon our muses of artistic inspiration as we progress through this world. Athena reminds us that we are all weavers in this life, working in threads of passion and inspiration at every opportunity and in all circumstances.

SPEAKING OF WEAVING . . .

A friend and I discovered a lovely word attributed to Michelangelo. It is *sprezzatura* and the definition is "the easy union of eye, hand, and brain to create worthy human works." He was referring to his art and the quality of creativity he values. I don't know who gets to decide what worthy is, but I love the idea of an easy union of senses, desires, and abilities. A lovely way to approach life, I think, an easy weaving of all that we are and all that we love, to create our lives. I can picture Athena and Michelangelo sipping espressos at a café, having a grand discussion on the topic.

YOU GUYS, ER . . . GALS

A few years ago I was asked to be a speaker at a film festival for teenaged girls. The girls spent the day in workshops watching and discussing films to learn about filmmaking and to talk about what they liked and why. Parents and guests were invited to join them for the end-of-the-day celebration, which I was to kick off with my hopefully inspiring speech. You never know the mood of your audience at the end of a long day, so I was prepared for anything. It is always tempting for me to try and get teens jazzed and get their rapt attention when I am in their midst. Teens get very good at masking their feelings, so surprises abound.

I launched into a rant about the marketing of movies, asking them if they realized that the under-eighteen female population was the dream market for film studios. And that their moms were the people TV show executives were hoping to woo. Why? Because girls and women spend money. I told the girls that they may not believe it, but that they held a great deal of

Make a Spectacle of Yourself!

Did anyone ever say to you, "Don't make a spectacle of yourself"? What is that all about? My immediate reaction has always been, "And why not?" So, let me get this straight —laughing out loud, wearing clothes we love, being visible and overtly joyful in the world, that's a bad thing? What is harmful to anyone about being big and bold and showy? Who gets hurt? Playing small is stingy. How dare you not share your beauty and joie de vivre with the world. Making a spectacle of yourself may simply mean speaking up for yourself for once. Our spectacles are our own and are relative to who we are and where we are in life. Give it a try.

power. What if a movie comes out and all the girls decide not to see it? And decide not to buy all the related tie-in products? Devastation for the studios and all the spin-off merchandisers. I held their attention, and I think made my point.

Some of the girls and a few of the moms came up to me afterward and said that they really appreciated my message to them. One woman told me that she liked the idea that I was telling the girls that they had more power in the world than they may have ever realized. Then came the "but": Did I realize that I used the term *guys* over and over again when addressing the girls? Ouch. She said I might want to think about that. I did, and I do think about it, and I have become sensitive to the fact that the phrase is everywhere and used in situations with all girls, all boys, and when it is mixed. The phrase has come to be accepted to mean everyone when used in addressing groups, but I would never want girls to think they are secondary to boys or that it is okay to lump them altogether under one category. Not to be too over the top with this, but I try to say "you all" when both genders are present and "you gals" when it is just us girls. Language is important. How we use it and what it means to us can be subtle and sometimes insidious if we don't pay attention.

It is good to notice not only how others talk to us but also how we talk to ourselves and each other; that is wise counsel at its best.

ON YOUR OWN: WWMD—WHAT WOULD MAME DO?

Athena and Auntie Mame would have either loved hanging out together or it would have been a disastrous combination of two bossy, smartypants gals. I love the idea though. Remember what Mame said: "Live, live, live! Life is a banquet, and most of you poor suckers are starving to death!" Now is your chance to counsel yourself through situations in a new way. It is time to stand up for yourself and to speak your mind. Go out there and make a bold new statement about who you are. There is no time or place for settling in this life; as someone once said, "Life isn't a dress rehearsal." Earn your Athena badge by doing something differently today. Do it from a place of wisdom and delight, not complacency or fear. Wear those purple tights you've been hanging on to. Say No to your usual routine and try something new. That can mean changing your daily or weekly habits or simply changing how you think about a certain situation or relationship. Athena was the patron of heroes. How can you better guide your own magical path? Walk right up to that banquet and fill up a couple of plates, and don't forget to try the calamari.

GROUP CELEBRATION

★) ★

Bee, Bee, Bee

I just had to put something craftsy in the book, and this is so much fun. Don't panic, those of you who think you may be creatively challenged, you just think you are and have to stop listening to that overactive brain of yours.

One of our lovely goddesses was getting married and someone (alright, it was me) had the idea to make a quilt for her. Though hardly an accomplished quilter, I am enthusiastic. I gave each gal in our goddess group a 12-inch square of muslin and told them to decorate it any way they wanted. When I first mentioned the idea for the project there were audible gasps, soon followed by excited questions. We had several gatherings where we worked together at our own goddess sewing bee. After the squares were complete I put them together and finished the quilt (yes, there was much cursing). It was great fun and so rewarding when we presented the bride with her quilt made with love. Each square revealed much about its maker and created a kaleidoscope of color and texture. Working together to create something makes for good, good energy to be born. Choose a project for your group, or bring your own works in progress and work on them together.

The Red Queen

Love her. Hot-tempered gal from *Alice Through the Looking Glass*. Insisted that most folks' heads needed to be separated from their bodies, immediately. We all have a bit of the Red Queen in us. She used to come out quite often when I drove in the city. Now I am more apt to appreciate the rush of energy that comes with a good dose of rage. Injustice and cruelty will always get to me. It is powerful, focused energy. We can channel it into our work, our workouts. We can even revel in the feeling of it dissipating as we shift our emotions. I am pretty clear on my triggers, but not always. Sometimes we are blind-sided by anger. It is our choice what to do with it.

RECIPES FOR ATHENA

The Natural Grocer is a lovely market in my neighborhood that is owned by a goddess and attended to by many lovely beings. The shop is filled with wholesome and organic goodies to satisfy every craving. Kathy, the goddess at the helm, is a dog person, so of course I liked her immediately. Her beautiful Newfie Maia used to lie on the air conditioning grate in the floor and graciously put up with endless comments and pets on her big soft head. Maia has since passed over to another realm, but her spirit lingers everywhere in the store. Kathy's puppy Newf Sophie still thinks the store is a giant smorgasbord set up just for her so she has to stay home for a bit longer. The kitchen goddesses create delicious lunches that feed folks from near and far. Thank goodness they are only a few blocks away from me.

Athena's Antipasti

One of my favorite dishes from Kathy's kitchen is a garlic lover's antipasti with garbanzo beans, caperberries, roasted red peppers, and a fabulous dressing. Kathy says, "A good antipasti is really all about the dressing." This delicious combination takes you right to the Mediterranean and to a little seaside café on a beautiful spring day. A perfect ode to our Athena, patroness of the city of Athens.

1 cup extra-virgin olive oil, $1/4$ cup reserved

1 cup garlic cloves, cut in halves or quarters

$1/2$ cup each balsamic vinegar and Bragg's Liquid Aminos

1 Tablespoon crushed garlic

Black pepper to taste

5 cups thickly sliced or quartered mushrooms

5 cups chick peas, cooked, drained, and ready to go

    (canned work just fine)

1 $1/2$ cups roasted red peppers

1 cup capers

$1/2$ cup caperberries (like capers on steroids, with long stems;
   available in gourmet shops and some grocery stores)

1 Tablespoon oregano

1 $1/2$ cups chopped Kalamata olives

Roast garlic cloves in the $1/4$ cup reserved olive oil until slightly golden in color, about 10 to 15 minutes in a 400°F oven. Set aside to cool. Save the oil.

Whisk together the vinegar, Bragg's, $1/2$ cup olive oil, crushed garlic, and salt. Add remaining ingredients together in a large bowl. Divide cooked garlic cloves in half and add to mix with half of the garlic oil. Save the rest again to adjust for taste before serving.

Pour dressing over the vegetable mix and toss gently but well. Chill and serve. Serves 10 to 12.

Cold Spicy Noodles

Athena was likely well traveled during military campaigns and may have liked the spices and flavors of the East. A great side dish or main course with a salad.

1 lb. egg noodles

2 Tablespoons sesame oil

3 Tablespoons tahini or peanut butter

2 teaspoons chili powder

1 1/2 Tablespoons finely chopped garlic

2 Tablespoons chili oil

2 Tablespoons light soy sauce

1 Tablespoon dark soy sauce

1 Tablespoon chili bean sauce

2 teaspoons finely chopped fresh ginger

1 teaspoon salt

2 teaspoons sugar

3 Tablespoons chopped scallions

Cook noodles in large pot of boiling water. Allow to cool. Toss with 1 tablespoon sesame oil. Mix in bowl remaining sesame oil and other ingredients. Pour over noodles and sprinkle scallions on top. Serves 4.

≈ HECATE ≈

QUEEN OF THE OUTCASTS

It is only with the heart that one can see rightly; what is essential is invisible to the eye.
—*Antoine de Saint-Exupéry,* The Little Prince

Hecate is the triple-faced lunar goddess who integrates not only our maiden, mother, and crone aspects but also our intuition for appreciating and integrating the many aspects of self—even and especially the ones that go against the standards of acceptability. The nighttime is her domain, and she watches over all those on the fringe of society. She regards all as equals, as she judges a person's heart, not her appearance or actions.

From Hecate we remember to diminish our prejudices about others and most important about ourselves. We are not too old, too fat, too poor, too late, too anything. There is great wisdom in who we are right now. She may not always give us the easiest road, and no doubt will challenge and push us to new appreciation and embodiment of our complex capacities for leading full, rich lives. Hecate demands a newfound acceptance of self and others. She offers guidance into decision making, using the wisdom from our youth, middle age, and old age, a state of grace and acceptance. There is no wrong choice at the crossroad when we know ourselves and respect ourselves for who we are right now. Listen to the quieter voices from within if they seem right. They won't let you down.

ROCK, PAPER, SCISSORS

We will never pass this way again. It is true. This very moment is gone in a blink. We are making our lives up as we go along. No one has ever been us at this moment, ever. No one will ever be again. So, why do we rely on that and those which came before us (even passing by five minutes ago) to dictate what comes next? Your life in this very moment is a first and a last; make it what you want. There are no *shoulds* and there are no wrong answers in life. Life and everything that goes with it is ours to make and ours alone to change. This moment is what we have to create with, like a handful of clay we can mold, an uncarved rock we can sculpt, or a whole piece of paper we can trim and shape.

Michelangelo said about his David, "I saw him in the marble and carved until I set him free."

And that is what we are all doing, too; carving and sculpting our life, revealing new pieces here and glimmering shapes there. All of our garden-variety selves combine to make up the life artisans we are. We are indeed artists sculpting our own paths. And we alone decide what goes where and how much red to use and when to lay the color on thicker, how loud to howl the blues, when to dance on the hot sand, and how soon to try finger painting in the dark.

MY WAY OR THE HIGHWAY

Well, well, well, you can tell I have been writing again because my eyebrows are over-plucked. Sometimes I scrutinize my eyebrows instead of writing, usually when I am sitting at my desk in search of inspiration. If only I could channel that energy into vacuuming or dusting. I didn't know *dust* could be a verb until recently, and even then it didn't get added to my repertoire of housecleaning talents. I like to wash dishes. That's about it. And doing laundry. Something about folding warm clothes and making big fluffy piles of them is very soothing. And I never had a yard before, so when I moved out of the city a few years ago I had to buy a lawnmower. I cut the grass in skirts and platform shoes. It makes my friends laugh and shake their heads. Most of them are amazed that I haven't chopped a toe off or rolled the thing into traffic. I can adapt, no problem, but I am going to do it my way. Just so you know.

We all have to do it our way, the way it makes us feel good,

Apropos of Nothing

I always loved that phrase. Definitely how my mind works. I can be talking away and suddenly and seemingly from nowhere a random unrelated thought will cross the highway and jump in front of my fast-moving train of a brain. It is truly apropos of nothing . . . or is it? This is where I think scientists first came up with the idea that we only use one iota of our brain capacity. We have got a lot going on in these heads of ours. I mean, look how much brain space we use over-thinking just about everything . . . our looks, our lives, our deficiencies in general. We tend to focus on these, the what-I-don't-haves versus the ohmygod-look-what-I-have. Apropos of nothing means not having to explain yourself to anyone for anything. Whatever you do is apropos of nothing other than what you want—the only way to go 'round in life, if you ask me.

and apologize to no one. Make no excuses for yourself or your choices, especially if they are different from most everyone else's. Be a rebel. The best part about making a decision about something is that you can always make another one if the first one doesn't feel right. And *feel* is the key word there—how *you* feel, not everyone else. The pursuit of our individuality and all that it means is our life's journey. We make choices all day, every day—small or large, paper or plastic, highway or back roads, crabby or joyful, we get to choose. Have fun with it. No two of us will come into this life, go through, and go out in the same way. That is the point. Be in relationship with all aspects of yourself, recognize and reclaim them. Let them all have a chance to make an appearance. Rediscover what it means to be a woman, what it means to be you.

MY FAVORITE OUTLAWS

My friend Judith recently called up to say that she was coming my way for her birthday. She was turning sixty-six. (Dame J: If you are upset with me for telling the world your age, I promise to make it right by taking you to Curtis's Barbecue Bus for ribs. We will make Ducky drive her big ol' station wagon. Ducky is

Led to Believe

Now there's an expression that always bothered me: "We are led to believe . . ." We are? Do we have to be led? We don't have to follow the beliefs of others. We don't need to be told what to believe, we know what we believe. We just have to remember. Ask yourself what you know, you'll find the answers. They're inside.

eighty—oops, did it again. I'll buy the beer, too.) Judith does something different every year for her birthday, like climb Mount Rainier or kayak somewhere extraordinary, which could mean not far beyond her backyard. For the past few years, she has climbed a local, not-so-small mountain every New Year's Day. She also threw a great birthday party for herself a few years back. This year she decided to come to the sea. She brought a pal and they played at the beach, and I met up with them later to dine on clams and crab cakes at a waterfront joint. Judith and I both love joints, and I am sure we would get in a whole lot of trouble if we ever traveled very far together. Ducky hasn't let a hip replacement slow her down and could out-hike or canoe most of us. She is an advocate for seniors and busier with causes and activities than most people half her age. These are gals who always speak their minds, who say what everyone else is thinking but isn't saying out loud, and have hearts the size of the Grand Canyon. I am lucky to have had many women in my life who remind me that we all have a place in this world and we don't have to be accepted by anyone but ourselves. Rock on, ladies.

★ Earning Your Hecate Badge ★

ON YOUR OWN: JUDGMENT JAR

At various times when I was growing up, Mom and Dad instituted the swear jar when we got a bit too free with our cursing. We had to put a quarter in the jar every time we swore. The lesson never lasted very long, but it did make us all more aware of the words we were using. So, now it is your turn to make a judgment jar. Each time you feel judgment rise in your throat, and especially when you verbalize it, put a quarter (or dollar) in the jar. The fine applies to any judgment you make about yourself as well as others. Notice how often you find yourself putting money in the jar. You may fill it up the first day. Just be aware.

GROUP CELEBRATION

Magic Women

In my goddess group we have created peace rituals and healing ceremonies that have been simple but powerful. Hecate is associated with dogs, illusion, and magic; this simple ritual works to let go of judgment or prejudice. Bring black or green candles to your next gathering. Black is Hecate's color, and green is the midpoint of the color spectrum, cools the blood, and invites harmony. Each woman places a candle in front of her. Light the candles. Ask yourself if there is any person you are in conflict with, or a conflict within yourself, that has slowed you down. As you continue to focus, put that conflict and any judgment that it brings up into the candle with your mind. Feel it leave your spirit and vanish into the flame. Realize that some conflicts can be healed, and others you will have to walk away from. It is your choice. Make it now in the silence. Close the ritual by visualizing the source of conflict in a golden light, and watch it drift away.

RECIPES FOR HECATE

Biscuits for Hecate's Hounds

I like to make a few big batches of dog biscuits to pass along to all my favorite canines at Christmas. I try to add ingredients that they will like and that will also be good for them—not always easy unless you have Labs around, because they will eat anything and everything, including the wooden spoon with batter on it if you leave it within nose's reach. All my dog pals really like these biscuits, except for Rocky—he spits them out. I'm working on a new recipe for him.

1 cup hot meat juices, gravy, or beef broth

1/3 cup olive oil

1/2 cup powdered milk

2 teaspoon maple syrup

1/2 teaspoon salt

1 egg, beaten

1/2 cup chopped parsley

3 cups oat or rice flour

1/3 cup ground flax seed

1 to 2 Tablespoons garlic, chopped (optional)

Preheat oven to 325°F. In a large bowl, stir together meat juices and olive oil. Add powdered milk, maple syrup, salt, flax seed, egg, and parsley and mix. Add flour half a cup at a time, mixing well between additions. I also add chopped garlic to batches going to beasties that I know will eat it. Knead mixture for 3 to 4 minutes, adding flour if necessary to make the dough stiff. Roll dough to $1/2$-inch thickness and cut out biscuits with bone-shaped cookie cutters or a variety of shapes. Place on greased cookie sheet and bake for about 50 minutes. Allow to cool and dry until hard. Makes 30 to 40 biscuits.

Scandalous Shrimp Scampi

Who doesn't love a good scampi? Add lots of garlic. Hecate won't mind.

4 Tablespoons olive oil

$3/4$ cup onion, diced

8 garlic cloves, chopped

28 medium shrimp, peeled and deveined

4 Tablespoons butter

$3/4$ cup dry white wine

Juice of 1 lemon

4 Tablespoons chopped scallions

4 Tablespoons parsley, finely chopped

1 cup tomatoes, chopped

$1/2$ cup cold water

4 Tablespoons flour

Salt and pepper to taste

Heat oil in a frying pan. Add the onions, garlic, and shrimp. Cook shrimp for 2 to 3 minutes. Add the butter, wine, lemon juice, scallions, parsley, and tomatoes. Cook until shrimp is pink.

Add the water. Sprinkle the flour slowly over the shrimp mixture while stirring. Add salt and pepper. Serve over spaghetti. Serves 4.

≈ PERSEPHONE ≈

MAMA'S GIRL

*When you stand with the blessings of your mother
and God, it matters not who stands against you.*
—Yoruba saying

Demeter, the nature goddess, sent her daughter Persephone to Earth to keep her away from the lusty gods above. They had started sniffing around, and Demeter wanted to keep Persephone out of sight. Nonetheless, as she wandered afield one day, Persephone was kidnapped by Pluto and brought to the underworld. Demeter was heartbroken at losing her daughter and made crops fail and brought eternal winter to the world. Don't mess with my little ones or a whole rash of misery will rain down upon you, in other words.

Finally a compromise was reached and Persephone was allowed six months in the underworld and six months with her mother above ground, during which the light and warmth of summer and spring returned. Persephone knows the worlds of darkness and light, and from both gains wisdom. She comes to her own understanding of fear and transcendence. We all have felt like a damsel in distress, and once in awhile it is nice to be

Love and Death and Taking It with You

As an epitaph for his friend, Sir Edmund Spenser wrote, "Death slew not him, but he made death his ladder to the skies." An easy and reassuring way to look at dying, with the hope and belief in heaven or somewhere beyond these earthly ties. Every culture has rituals associated with death, and often they are sacred and not to be altered. We all are eager to do our best to grant the dying wishes of those we love. Respecting their wishes about how and where their last days are spent often becomes a preoccupation. It gives us something to focus on and distracts us momentarily from their leaving and the questions of what comes next.

What comes next for them and what comes next for us? We are both sailing into uncharted territory. The person dying is sailing into the nonphysical and spiritual unknown. Those left behind may journey without a keel or with torn sails for awhile as an emotional void opens and we are forced to move into it and through it. And we will.

rescued. From Persephone we learn to ask for help when we need it and accept it when offered. You are already squirming, aren't you? Ask for help? Me? I don't need anyone's help. Sure thing, sister. Whatever you say.

Sometimes our girlfriends save us and sometimes it is a knight, but it is most powerful when we ourselves do the saving. Sometimes we have to touch the stove even though ten people have told us it's hot. Good to have someone there to bandage you up, but *you* have to ask for help. It really is fine to make choices that leave us hanging on the edge of the cliff—the view is amazing, isn't it? But once in awhile we have to put a hand out for assistance to get on solid ground again. I know it goes against our training to ask for help, but we must. It doesn't make us weak or any less independent. It connects us with others and the world and builds character.

DAMSEL IN DIS DRESS

It does make me feel good to have my guy friends look out for me, to worry a little bit about any new dog sniffing around. I have to say it even feels pretty great when they step in to diffuse a situation, get all puffed up and manly. Hey, when we are feeling vulnerable, sometimes it is nice to feel like the wolf is guarding the entrance to the cave. No one can get us. It is a primal

Life as Crate Training

I might know more about dogs than I do about people. At least I can relate so much in our people world to that of the canine universe. Dog land seems simpler, freer. Take crate training, for instance. My sister thinks that children should all be crate trained because it works so well for her dogs. She may only be half-kidding. Crate training is not cruel. It is a great way to teach a dog quickly and calmly not to pee on the new rug or shred the special-order running shoes. The pups get a cozy cave of their own, and you get a little peace of mind. We all need a safe spot and to know what the basic ground rules are.

Dogs are descended from wolves, and even though they ➳

fear and response. We all have it. It is okay to have someone look out for us, open the car door for us, keep tabs on us in a room full of people, to watch our backs. It is a safe way to feel vulnerable. We don't even have to be rescued, no one has to be beaten up or intimidated. We can just remember for a moment that someone else is keeping an eye on us, and that reprieve for a fleeting moment can give us hope and recharge our lovely, have been hanging out on our sofas for hundreds of years, way back when they were used to living in dens—small, enclosed spaces. This is why the crate works. So maybe we need to find our own crates when we are feeling a bit too vulnerable. A place within ourselves or a literal place that makes us feel safe. Sometimes being with other women to spend time, to listen, and to speak offers insight and encouragement and appreciation for ourselves and each other. To be able to say in response to someone telling you that you are not acting like yourself, "I must be acting like myself because I just did what I did; it wasn't someone else." Or, "This must be a part of who I am, and that is just fine." Maybe your goddess group will inspire or allow or encourage that response in you. Seems like a good place to crawl into and curl up.

romantic selves. It is lovely to be lovely. It is lovely to have someone notice us in the world and want to do something for us. We forget that; our little damsel selves need to be reminded now and again. Ask for help, and let people do things for you. We would do anything for anyone else. Why is so hard to ask for backup, a little special attention and notice?

TOUCHSTONE

A few years ago, in midwinter and sick with the flu, I stumbled out to my mailbox and found a squishy white package sitting on top. A letter was enclosed from a high school classmate explaining that inside were time capsules we had created in the seventh grade in 1974, not to be opened until February 2000. In among the pictures of the family cats and dogs, my first report card, and drawings of my sister and brother, was a letter from my mother. I recognized her handwriting instantly and had such a strong reaction that I had to put it on the table and walk away. My mother died many years ago, and I miss her every day. I stared at the letter, lit a fire, and curled up on the sofa with a blanket and read what she had written. My mother wished for me to have a happy and wonderful life and said how much she loved me. I could hear her voice come off the page and could picture her writing at the dining room table. It was likely after dinner, when the happy chaos of three teenaged children, several of their friends, and all the animals had settled a bit. I had a good long cry and then marveled at this gift that had been sent to me.

The letter is tucked inside my date book, so my mother is always with me, comforts me on hard days, and reminds me how extraordinary life indeed is. There she is still looking out for me. Sometimes help and inspiration comes from far away or out of thin air, but it is there no matter what. Silent asking is just as powerful as saying it out loud. Don't barricade the door when help arrives; welcome it in.

★) ★

The Cats in the Hats

On one weekend goddess getaway we broke into the hat cupboards at the house in which we were staying. Next thing I knew we were singing and dancing in boaters, bowlers, and pith helmets. It was fun to see what hats we gravitated toward. We got to play at new personas and reveled in the freedom from inhibitions for a little bit of time.

Give Hat Night or Costume Night a try with your gals. Each person can bring one, and then you can all trade when you get there. Or pick a theme for the evening and build outfits around them. You will be laughing and dancing in no time.

★ Earning Your Persephone Badge ★

ON YOUR OWN: SAY IT

You need help. Look around your living space. Surely there is some project that requires assistance. What about that huge piece of furniture that you would prefer go against the other wall or the picture that needs to be rehung? And all you have to do is ask. People really do like being asked to help. If they say No you have to let it go, but unless you're asking them for help with something illegal or for a favor that will put them in harm's way, you shouldn't have too much trouble finding someone to pitch in. So earn your Persephone badge by asking for help with some pesky task that has been weighing on your mind or for an introduction to someone you are interested in or want to get to know because they work in a field you are interested in. Favors don't all have to involve labor. People love being asked for their expertise; it makes everyone feel good.

RECIPES FOR PERSEPHONE

Bloody Marvelous Virgin Marys

Persephone is one of the virgin Greek goddesses, so it is only fitting to offer a virgin concoction. I'm not saying you can't augment it with any liquid of your choice, however. They are spicy and hot and a right hair of the dog either way. Just the thing for a gal stuck in the underworld all winter.

16 oz. tomato juice, chilled

1 teaspoon prepared horseradish

Fresh black pepper to taste

Sea salt

2 teaspoons Worcestershire sauce

2 fresh limes

10 drops (or more!) hot sauce of your choice

Ice

Pickled dill green beans or long wedge of cucumber

Chill glasses for at least an hour.

Combine tomato juice, horseradish, pepper, dash or two of salt, Worcestershire sauce, juice of one lime, hot sauce, and a handful of ice in a cocktail shaker. Shake until well mixed. Strain into glasses. Run a small quarter-lime around the edge of each glass, toss in when done. Add a pickled bean or cucumber wedge, and bottoms up! This is a recipe for two but can be easily altered; just figure about 8 oz. of tomato juice per glass and adjust other ingredients to taste.

Oh Mama! Moisturizing Oatmeal Scrub

Every gal needs to moisturize her lovely visage. The following is a fun recipe to make with your goddesses. Slather it on your gorgeous faces for a beauty regimen after dinner.

> 1 cup rolled oats, ground in the blender until fine, makes $1/2$ cup
>
> $1/2$ cup dry powdered milk
>
> 1 Tablespoon apricot kernel oil or other facial quality oil
>   (health food store)
>
> 2 drops essential oil (lavender, geranium, and so on)
>
> $1/2$ cup water

Transfer oats to a bowl and mix with dry powdered milk. Stir in oils and water. Apply paste to face, hands, feet, or legs, and gently scrub. Leave on for 15 minutes or so and then rinse off for silky, radiant skin. Can be refrigerated for up to five days. Makes about $3/4$ cup.

≈ SPIDER WOMAN ≈

GRANNY WISDOM

Nobody sees a flower—really—it is so small it takes time—we haven't time—and to see takes time, like to have a friend takes time.
—Georgia O'Keeffe

Spider Woman belongs to the Hopi Indians of the Southwest. She is a part of their creation story. With patience and insight, Spider Woman brought light to the new world. She traveled from east to west, north to south, and back again, trailing her web, and created the sun, the moon, and the star people with their crystal eyes. She returned with the gift of fire. She created people from all the different colored clay in the earth and attached her thread to the top of each one's head. This is the thread of wisdom, our connection to her sense and understanding. When we remember this connection, we have access to the enlightenment of those who came before us.

We can learn so much from our grandmothers. I hope you have remembered to ask yours their stories over the years. Both of mine are gone, and I still have so many questions about their lives and the times they grew up in. My grandmothers could not have been more different. My dad's mother was tiny with red hair. She and the family fled Czechoslovakia in 1939, and via England and Cuba, finally landed in New York. She never lost her accent. Granny had graduated from law school in Prague, in the first class to graduate women, but never practiced in this country. She was never judgmental, welcomed questions and stories about life and love, and offered quiet wisdom. I never heard bitterness in her voice about leaving her country and all that she knew.

My mom's mother was 5 feet, 10 inches tall. Her father was a French count and her mother an activist and dancer. My grandmother was one of five children and grew up in Europe and the United States. She was an artist and avid gardener and taught me to cherish color and beauty in all forms. I am still learning from them both and carry them with me always.

Amazing Grace

I was hiking in the desert with some folks and wandered a little bit away by myself. I paused to look down at the ground and spied a tarantula ambling along in the vast open space. I was stunned to see the beautiful creature making its way across the terrain. This was her land, after all. I was just a visitor. Seeing animals and insects in their natural habitat is intoxicating, a real rush for me. What gives you a rush of delight?

MRS. MAPLE

A big ol' tree also kept an eye on me when I was growing up. We left the city for the country every summer, traveling to a small town several hours away. The house was at the top of a hill at the end of a long dirt road. It was cozy and had big fields across from it where my sister, brother, and I played for hours. We named the mossy area at the edge of the woods Fairyland, and we loved to sit and run our fingers along the soft ground and make up stories about the little people that lived there.

The house was watched over by an enormous tree. She had stood there for a hundred years already by the time we arrived. I sometimes wondered if she was tired, holding her branches out to the world for so long. For many summers it took all three of us together to get our arms all the way around her. She was definitely the kind of tree you wanted to hold onto and run your fingers over her bark. She was magical. I felt like she protected us. I read and daydreamed and sometimes cried under her vast canopy, but I always felt better when I sat beneath her thick branches and leaned against her trunk. We all (the dogs too) picked blueberries nearby, and she kept an eye on the comings and goings. She didn't even object to a hammock secured around her middle one year. Every thunderstorm we worried about her as the lightning crackled and flashed, but she stood still throughout the years, silent and immovable.

Mom eventually sold the house to Sandy, who loved it, and everyone was happy. After Mom died Sandy and I stayed in touch off and on over the years. Not long ago she called and told me that the tree was sick and couldn't be saved. It was going to be cut down. She just wanted my brother and sister and me to know. We were all heartbroken. I told her that we called her Mrs. Maple, and we both cried. I felt like I was losing an important guardian from childhood, something everlasting. Mrs. Maple was a goddess, a strong, comforting, beautiful being. We can find beauty and strength everywhere we look, everywhere we are, and from any everlasting moment of our lives.

GROUP CELEBRATION

★) ★

Talking Stick

Talking sticks have Native American origins. The talking stick identifies the person in the group who has the permission to speak. I originally did this activity with a group of teenaged girls I was involved with in a mentoring project. We were in a place of conflict in the group, and as a result communication had all but shut down. I was looking for a way to get us back on track, to give everyone a chance to be heard. The talking stick allows time and silence for reflection and understanding.

You'll need a good-sized stick or dowel, about two feet long. A real live stick from the great outdoors is optimal, one that has already fallen to the ground. Don't go pulling branches off trees, please. My talking stick is white birch, because it is my favorite tree. I found it when I was hiking. All sticks are pretty great. Pry one out of your dog's mouth if you have to. The beasties are very good at finding sticks out there in the world if you need some help. Trade her for a tennis ball—a nice ABC (already been chewed) one—that usually works.

Ask the other gals in your group to each bring a strip or two of brightly colored cloth to your next gathering. It can be an old nightgown that they tear up or a remnant from the sewing basket or even a ribbon. The strip should be long enough to tie around the stick (8 to 12 inches works well). Some folks can bring extras along for others, too.

As you pass the stick around the group, have each woman tie a piece of material onto the stick and say, "Tonight I honor . . . She gave me . . . ."

You can keep the stick and use it to open gatherings and to pass when sharing information, or use as a centerpiece and reminder that all of the women who have come before us are with us always.

★ **Earning Your Spider Woman Badge** ★

ON YOUR OWN: STORYTELLING

There is something extraordinary about women who have lived longer than we have. It can be such a lovely connection to spend time with them. If you have grandmas or great aunts or elder friends still living, think about spending some time with them and asking them about their lives. Or there might be an older woman in your neighborhood whom you haven't had the chance to engage for longer than a smile. People usually love to tell their stories, even if they are shy at first. Earn your Spider Woman badge by honoring an woman elder in your life. If she is living, then make a point to call or visit and ask her to tell you her stories. If she is gone physically, then spend some time with her in your mind. What did you learn from her? Inherit from her? How did she impact your life? How would you like to honor her?

RECIPES FOR SPIDER WOMAN

When I was in film school in Santa Fe, my pal Amy and I lived about a block away from each other on Canyon Road. My apartment, which was about as big as my desk, was in Gypsy Alley. How could I not live there with a name like that? It had the tiniest kiva fireplace in it too, which was the clincher for me signing the lease. It is now an art gallery. The high desert is still a magical part of the world for me. It was where I learned to love green and red chiles and where I was first introduced to the Spider Woman legend.

Sometimes on clear winter nights, way back when, Amy and I would head down to a restaurant about halfway between us, sit at the bar, and order the green chile turkey soup. It was spicy and hearty and so delicious. They served it with garlic toast that was just the perfect touch. I can smell the piñon fires and feel the crisp cold air just thinking about it.

Gypsy Alley Green Chile Turkey Soup

This soup definitely cures what ails you. I love the heat and earthy green chiles; fresh roasted are without compare. I've changed things around a bit with my recipe; you can make this soup your own, too. Turn up or down the fire in it, and add or subtract vegetables to your heart's desire. This soup is good the day you make it and even better the next and the next.

Chiles

5 or 6 green chiles (Hatch or Anaheim chiles if you can get them,
  or 2 cans roasted, if you have to)

Soup

1 cooked turkey breast available at the supermarket (or you can
  buy a small turkey and use the bones to make the broth after
  you cook it and remove the meat)

2 cloves garlic, chopped

1 big handful of fresh parsley, chopped

1 medium yellow onion, coarsely chopped

1 cup chopped carrot

1 cup chopped butternut squash

1 red pepper, chopped

1 fresh jalapeño (optional), stem and seeds removed

1 Tablespoon olive oil

2 cups (at least) homemade or purchased broth

1 cup white wine

1 can whole tomatoes, drained and coarsely chopped

1 cup basmati brown rice

Parmesan cheese for grating

$1/2$ lemon

Salt to taste

To roast chiles: Place oven rack on top setting. Place a sheet of aluminum foil across the rack. Place chiles on foil and turn broiler to high. Turn chiles several times, until they are charred and black on all sides. It won't be a pretty sight, but it makes them tastier and easier to peel. Open oven, being careful not to inhale as you bend down—you can get a big dose of chile smoke, which can irritate eyes and lungs. Using tongs, place chiles in a paper bag, seal, and put aside for 20 minutes or more. It should now be easy to peel the charred skin from the chiles. Remove the stems and most of the seeds and chop.

Sauté the garlic, parsley, onion, carrots, squash, red pepper, and jalapeño in olive oil over medium heat for a few minutes until onion just starts to get soft.

Add the broth, wine, and tomatoes (and the turkey bones if you have them). Make sure there is enough liquid to cover the other ingredients. Add more broth or water if necessary. Turn up the heat and allow the mixture to boil.

Reduce heat and add the chiles and rice. Cover and simmer for at least one hour.

Remove the turkey bones and add the cooked turkey torn or cut into bite-sized pieces. Squeeze the lemon into the pot. Stir and salt to taste. Add a few grates of cheese before serving in festive bowls. Serve with warm flour tortillas or garlic bruschetta. Serves 6 to 8.

Sweet Potato Pancakes

These are earthy and make delicious appetizers.

1 large sweet potato, peeled

1 small white onion

1 egg, lightly beaten

3 Tablespoons flour

$1/8$ teaspoon nutmeg

$1/4$ cup cranberry relish

In a food processor, shred the sweet potato and onion. Squeeze out any moisture. Transfer to a large bowl and combine with egg, flour, and nutmeg.

Heat a griddle or cast iron frying pan, and lightly butter it. Drop sweet potato batter by tablespoons onto surface and flatten slightly with the back of a spoon. Cook until golden; then turn and cook until other side is also golden. Transfer to paper towels. Arrange pancakes on a plate, and garnish each with a small dollop of cranberry relish. Makes about 20.

≈ HESTIA ≈

THE HOMEGIRL

Turn soft and lovely any time you have a chance.
—Jenny Holzer, artist

Hestia is the keeper of the hearth and home, the creator of our safe harbors, and the protector of our core selves. She is us tending to our internal fires, our spirit. Her name according to Plato means "the essence of things." Hestia reminds us to make our hearth and home a sanctuary. Our physical home provides shelter to our inner home, to our essence. Be with others who tend these fires, remove yourself from those who do not. Yes to those who fan and ignite the fire, but No to the ones wanting to extinguish it. Turn your attention to home. What does it means for you and how you want it to be?

EDDIE

Growing up in our house was like growing up in a youth hostel. There were the three of us kids, and usually a few extras at dinner time and on weekends. We had the house where everyone hung out. Mom always cooked enough for all the extras. We had two dogs and four cats, although sometimes we had three dogs because Eddie was visiting. Eddie was like a Vegas lounge singer in a dog suit. He was a smooth-talking medium-sized Golden Retriever mix who showed up at the door every few months and stayed for a week or so before heading off again. He strolled into our house each time like he had just gone to the store for a pack of smokes and hadn't been gone but a minute.

Eddie had a tag on his collar, so Mom called the number the first time he appeared and said to the man who answered the phone, "I think we have your dog." The mysterious man responded nonchalantly, "Okay, send him home when he feels like it. His name is Eddie." Eddie lived all the way across town, in a neighborhood separated by many busy city streets. The big park just down from our house may have been the lure to our neighborhood. Eventually, after Eddie had shown up several times, Mom would call the number on the tag and say, "Eddie is here. We'll send him home in a few days." Eddie let Mom know when it was time to hit the road. He hung out at the door more and just got fidgety. Eddie arrived on foot but always left in a cab. Of course he did. Mom was horrified at the idea of Eddie heading off across town on his own, despite the fact that he had clearly been out and about in the city for quite some time. Mom called Boston Cab and explained to them about the passenger they would be picking up. I'm sure she was a big tipper. Sooner or later the dispatcher would find a willing driver, and a cab would round the corner onto our street. The whole family would gather out front when the cab pulled up. We waved as Eddie hopped in and sat upright on the back seat as he was chauffeured back to his other life. He looked very much at home in the back of a taxi. I imagined Eddie was pulling this scam on people all over the city. He probably rarely spent much time at his real home.

Mom took in strays, anyone or thing who showed up at the door. Some may have called her naive. We were sometimes confused and even occasionally angry when she hired cleaning people who didn't clean but drank coffee at the dining room table all morning reading the newspaper and vacuumed in the nude during the hot summer months (a bit much for teenagers to handle), or babysitters/struggling actors looking for a break who almost poisoned us with raw chicken, and contractors, just released from prison, who painted the windows shut and stole all her jewelry. That was my mom, amused by and interested in all those she

> ### Reality Check
>
> Just a brief thought about reality. . . . Reality is what you believe, not what someone else has told you to believe. You can change your reality anytime, day or night. It's what you want to see, feel, taste, touch, and hear that matters. That part is up to you.

came across. She welcomed each and every one of us in out of
the rain, muddy paws and all.

GROUP CELEBRATION

★) ★

Shake and Bake

A group of gals baking bread together sounds warm and cozy
and Sunday afternoon-ish and evokes good feelings of abundance, don't you think? So, in honor of Hestia, plan a gathering
on a weekend day so that you will have plenty of time to bake
and visit. Bread dough has to rise, so you will have to do part of
the preparations ahead of time. A delicious bread recipe follows.

★ Earning Your Hestia Badge ★

ON YOUR OWN:
THE ENERGY OF COLOR

This is a perfect chance to focus on your abode and putting things in place to make it as cozy as you want. It's a good time to tackle creative projects that will feather your nest.

Find lovely fabric in all the colors you love, wear them, dance with them, or use them as tablecloths or drape them over a chair. Color is so significant in our lives. Colors effect our moods and motivations. The seven primary colors are matched by seven notes on a scale and seven planets in the solar system. So, add a little color to your world. Paint a door red, or a ceiling blue. Place pink azaleas in your bedroom or daisies in your kitchen. Buy bright new pillows for the sofa or your bed. Use the energy of color to impact your spirit and your dreams. Become aware of the colors you are drawn to.

RECIPES FOR HESTIA

My friend Lisa is a chef and the former creator/owner of the wonderful On the Park restaurant in the South End of Boston. She is the hardest-working gal I know and a true Hestia in spirit. I first met her when I lived across the street from the restaurant and walked my dog past her kitchen every day on the way to the park. Lisa gave out biscuits to all the dogs that strolled by with their people. My beast was one of many that would sled-dog over to Lisa's back door each time we passed by. Lisa is one of those over-the-top good energy people you just want to be around. Dogs think so too. She is a sublime cook, and the atmosphere in her restaurant was electric. I was swept up into a magical dining experience each time I was there.

On the Park Bread

The following recipe is for the delicious bread Lisa served at the restaurant.

$1^1/2$ Tablespoons sugar

$1^1/2$ Tablespoons granular yeast

$4^1/2$ cups warm water

3 cups all purpose flour

2 Tablespoons Kosher salt

$^1/_8$ cup olive oil

$^1/_2$ cup flour for rolling dough out

Place sugar and yeast in a bowl, add 1 cup warm water (90–100°F) and mix lightly. Let sit in a warm area until the yeast starts to grow, about 15 minutes.

Add the 3 cups flour, *then* the salt, and then the olive oil (if you add the salt first you will kill the yeast and the dough won't rise). Mix ingredients with your hands until the mixture forms a ball of dough. Place dough on a lightly floured surface and knead for 10 to 15 minutes until dough has a light sheen and is holding its shape. Transfer to a lightly oiled, large bowl, and cover with an oiled piece of plastic wrap. Place in refrigerator for 24 hours.

Preheat oven to 375°F. Remove dough from bowl and cut into equal pieces (3 loaves on average). Place $^1/_2$ cup of flour on a flat surface; take each loaf and push down and roll the dough tightly into a cigar-like shape. Repeat with the remaining dough. Place loaves on an oiled sheet pan and place in oven. Bake until bread is golden brown—45 minutes to 1 hour. Let bread rest 10 minutes before you eat it, or allow it to completely cool and wrap it in plastic wrap.

Pickled Grapes

One summer my goddess gals rented a seaside cottage for the weekend. We found this recipe in the kitchen. Pickled grapes sounds a little funky, I know, but they are really delicious and great in salads or just on their own. Pickling and canning are such great homegirl activities.

> 2 lbs. seedless red grapes
>
> 2 cups rosé or raspberry wine vinegar
>
> 1 cup dry red wine
>
> 1 1/4 cups sugar
>
> 4 whole cloves, or more
>
> 1 cinnamon stick
>
> 6 cardamom seeds, crushed
>
> 1 sprig fresh tarragon

Place grapes in 2-quart jar. Place remaining ingredients in saucepan over medium heat; stir until sugar dissolves. Cool slightly. Pour over grapes. Let marinate 2 days. Invert jar several times over the time. Keeps for 10 days in refrigerator. Makes 1 quart.

≈ SAINT LUCY ≈

LADY OF LIGHT

Unless you believe, you will not understand.
—Saint Augustine

Lucy is the patron saint of vision, visionaries, and writers. I have a special fondness for her. Her story has been told many times and in many ways. She was originally the pagan goddess Lucina, the goddess of light. Lucy of Syracuse lived in the third century in Sicily. She was born into a wealthy family. They were big into arranged marriages then. Lucy wanted to devote her life to God and had no interest in the pagan bachelor her mother chose for her. She stalled the marriage, and in the process of praying for guidance at the tomb of Saint Agatha, she also asked for help with her mother's blood disease. The disease was cured, and her mother allowed Lucy to distribute riches to the poor. The disgruntled fiancée was not pleased with the marriage being postponed, nor with his future wealth being given away. He sought revenge. Guards came to take Lucy away to force her into prostitution, but they found that they could not move her, not even with oxen. At some point her eyes were put out and an attempt made to set her on fire. Divine intervention extinguished the flames and restored her sight before she was finally stabbed and killed. Good God, what you had to endure to become a saint.

From Lucy we find strength in our vision and clarity of our insight into ourselves and others. Look into the corners. Look at the different light, the long winter shadows, the quality of reflection. Can we see differently and therefore know ourselves more clearly? What are our beliefs and what are we committed to? Is there a new vision possible, a new way to see life within ourselves? Can we be as committed to that new vision as Lucy was to her devotion to God? Lucy is often depicted with a reflection of her eyes on a plate she is holding in her hands. What do your eyes reflect to or about you? Where is the focus of your vision? Does it need refining or refocusing?

LIFE IN TECHNICOLOR

Don't you just love the part in *The Wizard of Oz* when Dorothy's house lands in Munchkinland and she opens her black and white door to reveal a vibrant Technicolor world? Magical. I often feel that way when I am out and about in the world. Don't you love to be outdoors? The world outside our door is just waiting for us to step out and greet it. It may be challenging, but ultimately, it will never disappoint you. We're the only ones who can do that. Each and every time we step out, we have the

Seven Deadly Sins?

A local writer and director put out a call for short plays, asking folks to choose one of the seven deadly sins as the theme. Great idea, I thought, and then realized it had been awhile since I checked the sins on the list. So I looked them up. They are, in case anyone else has also forgotten: pride, envy, lust, wrath, sloth, gluttony, greed. I don't know about you, but some of these are a few of my favorite pastimes. These are sins? I think we should redo the list.

chance to see everything in a new light, with new eyes. It is our choice what we focus on each and every time. Is it going to be large and small acts and visions of beauty that hold your gaze or will it be meagerness and offensive sights?

TITANIC GLASS

The cup holders in my car are filled with sea glass and stones and feathers and other found objects. They hold all the touchstones and necessities a gal needs when out in the world. Alright, so there are dog biscuits and many, many lipsticks in there, too, but you can never have enough treats nearby, cosmetic or otherwise. You never know who you might come across and what shade of lipstick your mood might call for. Passengers just have to hold their coffees and water bottles in their hands when riding with me. I see things and I want to pick them up and feel them and always wonder where they came from. Mostly these treasures are on the ground, on the beach, or in the woods.

I love to look at how the sea changes and softens and tears apart all that she gets in her clutches. Bottles and jars are shattered and then transformed into smooth, opaque treasures only to be discovered months and years later, hundreds of miles away from their starting place. Sometimes I make up origin stories to go with what I discover on the sand. Once I found a piece of fancy cut glass that had been claimed by the ocean. The intricate details were still visible, yet it was just a fragment. I decided that it was from a wine glass on the *Titanic,* and pictured a woman in a beautiful blue gown laughing and sipping from it once upon a time. Her dress was sprinkled with sparkles and matched her eyes in color and depth. Her dashing companion whispered something slightly dangerous, something suggestive, and she laughed just a bit too loud in response. Her hand held the ornate glass aloft as she paused between sips to assess the man's intent. That is what I see. That is the story I read in this small piece of crystal brought in on the tide. Everything and everyone has stories connected to them. We can change them anytime we want. It's just a matter of how you want to see things, how you want to see yourself.

★ **Earning Your Saint Lucy Badge** ★

ON YOUR OWN:
RIGHT HERE, RIGHT NOW

Welcoming love and adventure into your life can begin with small tastes of newness. This is our time to shine and dance and play, to love deeply, starting with ourselves. When someone tells you that you look beautiful or are so smart and wonderful, just hear it and say thank you. When we say it to our lovelies, we mean it. We have to accept it when they say it to us. Believe them and then believe it yourself. Love who and where you are this instant. If that is a stretch, then discover one thing that you can love about yourself—your ability to make people smile, your beautiful feet, your physical strength, how you handle so many tasks at once, the light from your eyes. If that pushes your limits of believability right this minute, then do one thing today that will remind you of who you are right now. See yourself in a whole new light. Rediscover and remember. There are no wrong answers. Earn your Saint Lucy badge by making a list of all your discoveries.

GROUP CELEBRATION

★) ★

Mirror, Mirror

Sometimes we need to adjust our mirrors. With the help of others we can tilt them in a little different light from the same angle we've been staring at forever. And voila! It is a whole new view.

After you have settled in and feasted or visited for a bit, get a pack of 3 x 5 cards or cut up pieces of paper and put them in the middle of the table or floor. Next have people write down lots of positive adjectives like *delicious, beautiful, charming, brilliant, sexy, daring,* and such. When you have gathered a good-sized pile, put them in a hat or a basket and mix them up. Go around the group and pick one or two words at a time and create a sentence using the words you chose. "When I look in the mirror I see (fill in your own name), a courageous, beautiful woman." You can choose words for yourself and then for each other. Good feelings will bloom, and we will remember to appreciate the woman looking back at us in the mirror.

RECIPES FOR SAINT LUCY

Saint Lucy's feast day is December 13. St. Lucia's Day in Sweden marks the beginning of Christmas celebrations. Buns are baked in Saint Lucy's honor each feast day.

Every Christmas morning my mother made a coffee cake to accompany the present-opening frenzy. I never got her recipe, but the one following is pretty close and delicious. My dad loves the crunchy topping, known in our family as the "gooky gook."

Christmas Coffee Cake

It seems perfect to offer in Saint Lucy's honor a recipe close to my mom's. You can mix the whole thing the night before and then pop it in the oven in the morning.

Cake

2 cups sifted flour

1 teaspoon baking powder

1 teaspoon baking soda

1 teaspoon ground cinnamon

$1/2$ teaspoon salt

$2/3$ cup butter, at room temperature

1 cup sugar

$1/2$ cup brown sugar

2 eggs

1 cup buttermilk

Topping

$1/2$ cup brown sugar

$1/2$ cup walnuts

$1/2$ teaspoon cinnamon

$1/4$ teaspoon nutmeg

Sift flour, baking powder, baking soda, cinnamon, and salt together. In a large bowl, cream butter, sugar, and brown sugar until fluffy. Add the eggs to the butter mixture one at a time, beating after each addition. Add the dry ingredients alternately with the buttermilk. Spread in a greased and floured 9 x 13-inch pan.

With a fork, combine the topping ingredients in a small bowl and sprinkle over the batter. Refrigerate overnight or for 12 hours. Bake in a preheated oven at 350°F for 45 minutes. Serves 6.

≈ LILITH ≈

SOLO GIRL

*[Wo]Men are wise in proportion, not to their
experience, but to their capacity for experience.*
—*James Boswell,* Life of Samuel Johnson (1791)

This is just about my favorite myth. Lilith was Adam's first wife
and quite independent. Adam was a bit of a brute, not long on
hygiene nor manners in the ways of love. Lilith refused to sleep
with him and took off on her own. All hell broke loose, and the
powers that be found Eve to take her place, hoping she might be
more docile. Thousands of years later, we are still expected to
couple up. Not everyone thrives that way, however. Some gals
need to fly solo for awhile or always. Let me just tell you that
Lilith went off and cavorted with all sorts of characters and
seemed to have a pretty good time. So, what if we decide to do
it differently, to stay single and take care of ourselves only? Did
you hear a gasp? Ignore it. From Lilith we remember to honor
our choices about independence and freedom from expectations. Doing it our way means whatever way feels right for us.

STONE SOUP

A great deal has been theorized about the idea of fight or flight in humans when faced with fear or dangerous situations. That might apply to men, but it doesn't work for women. Our response to adversity is to handle it. We don't fight or flee, we just deal. It goes way, way back to the days of yore (or before, whenever that is), when mastadons roamed the Earth and women were already looking for a way to get out of the cave for

Woman of the Phoenix

Vince Bell wrote a beautiful song by that title. Nanci Griffith sings it so that it makes you let go a big wild sigh when you hear it. My favorite line is the one about wandering and being wooed. To wander and be wooed? I have to say that sounds pretty delicious. When I hear the song I find myself sitting outside on a summer night with so many stars just inches above my head. I am in love with the world and it is loving me back. I adore the days and nights when we go out into life and just marvel at everyone and everything. When we woo the universe and it woos us right back. It is all too irresistible.

a bit. If Og went off to hunt for meat, got chewed on by a saber-toothed tiger and didn't return, Mrs. Neanderthal still had to make soup out of rocks. The little ones were hungry. She had to make do. We have never been ones to roll over easily. We gathered fruits and berries, tended the fire, and carried on. Maybe we hunted, too. We are caretakers and providers; it is just what we do or have done for millions of years. Millions of years is a long time for patterns to get ingrained. In the face of any crisis our reaction is to make food, to comfort and provide. Isn't it the very first thing we think of when someone is ill or there is a crisis: "Let's bring some food." It is what we can do and do so well. It says that we care. It makes us feel useful and needed. Wouldn't it be lovely if we gave as much care to ourselves as we do to everyone else? You don't have to abandon everyone. Just make sure you take care of people and details because you want to, not because you have some notion that you have to.

PUPPY FEAR PERIODS

Puppies go through times when they are growing, and they grow soooo much more quickly than people do that everything is a little bit scary. They may startle more than usual or become shy. The world seems too big and loud and confusing. Sounds logical to me. They are packing seven or so years into every one

The Original Story . . . of Stone Soup

Once upon a time, somewhere in Eastern Europe, there was a great famine. People jealously hoarded whatever food they could find, hiding it even from their friends and neighbors. One day a peddler drove his wagon into a village, sold a few of his wares, and began asking questions as if he planned to stay for the night.

"There's not a bite to eat in the whole province," he was told. "Better keep moving on."

"Oh, I have everything I need," he said. "In fact, I was thinking of making some stone soup to share with all of you." He pulled an iron cauldron from his wagon, filled it with water, and built a fire under it. Then, with great ceremony, he drew an ordinary-looking stone from a velvet bag and dropped it into the water.

By now, hearing the rumor of food, most of the villagers had come to the square or watched from their windows. As the ➡

of ours. Can you imagine being twelve one day and seventeen a few weeks later? I think I would step cautiously into the world on those days, too. We need to be gentle with them and ourselves when we are going through these fear cycles.

peddler sniffed the "broth" and licked his lips in anticipation, hunger began to overcome their skepticism.

"Ahh," the peddler said to himself rather loudly, "I do like a tasty stone soup. Of course, stone soup with *cabbage*—that's hard to beat."

Soon a villager approached hesitantly, holding a cabbage he'd retrieved from its hiding place, and added it to the pot. "Capital!" cried the peddler. "You know, I once had stone soup with cabbage and a bit of salt beef as well, and it was fit for a king."

The village butcher managed to find some salt beef . . . and so it went, through potatoes, onions, carrots, mushrooms, and so on, until there was indeed a delicious meal for all. The villagers offered the peddler a great deal of money for the magic stone, but he refused to sell and traveled on the next day. And from that time on, long after the famine had ended, they reminisced about the finest soup they'd ever had.

We go through our own puppy fear periods when we are trying new things on for size. They don't last long usually, can be quite fleeting really, but very real and quite powerful nonetheless. If you make a decision in your life that goes against the grain, an extra dose of courage may be necessary. So, if you are trying to call upon a goddess aspect that has been dormant for a bit or bringing a new one to the surface, you may experience puppy fear. I doubt you will piddle on the floor, but you sure might feel like it. You may be shy suddenly or lose confidence momentarily. Try not to let it dissuade you from forging ahead. Gal pals can come in handy right about now. Try on a mood and see where it takes you. Try on a new perspective and see what is inspired from your new vantage point. If you can get through to the other side of the fear, you will feel magnificent.

ON YOUR OWN: GOOD DATE

This is about you being okay on your own. I was doing a reading recently and was talking about going to the movies by myself, and I heard a woman actually gasp in the audience. She told me later that she couldn't possibly imagine going to the movies by herself. People would pity her and think she was pathetic. Ohmygoddess. Haven't we been over this before? Who cares what other people think of you? And it is just as likely that some are thinking how cool you are and some how lucky you are that you don't have to fight for the armrest or make small talk before the previews or discuss the film afterward. Try taking yourself on a date. I bet you'll find that you are quite good company. Bring a book or your journal to a restaurant or some work you have to do. The wait staff will take good care of you, and you can enjoy your meal in silence. Earn your Lilith badge by doing something alone you have never done before, or at least not in a long time.

GROUP CELEBRATION

★) ★

Making Space

Those same old, same old lame-o skeletons are just taking up space in your closet, aren't they? Time to clean them out and make space for possibility. Take clothes to your favorite charitable organization, or have a yard sale. You will be surprised by all the room you will create for your life by getting rid of stuff. I was moving a few years ago and asked all my pals to help me. What troupers. It was an unseasonably cold day and rainy off and on, but there they were very early on a Saturday. It is so much more fun to do it with other people.

Have a goddess yard sale. Pick one location to have the sale and corral the neighbors in the area, too. It is such a kick to get money for things that you don't use any more. Keep the money or give it to charity. Have you stopped wearing suits or dress clothes? It feels great to donate clothes to a women's shelter and know they will be boosting a fellow goddess' confidence.

RECIPES FOR LILITH

Stone Soup

Remember the story about the stone soup? (See the sidebar called "The Original Story . . . of Stone Soup" on page 150.) That is exactly what you and your goddess group will do. Each one bring an ingredient for soup and put it all together when you gather. It can be all vegetables or with meat as well. I am sure it will be wonderful. Don't forget the magic stone.

Hot Deviled Artichoke Dip

Serve the following with good multiseed crackers or toasted pita.

> Two 14 oz. cans artichoke hearts in water, drained and chopped
>
> 1 cup mayonnaise
>
> 1 cup Parmesan cheese
>
> 3 chopped hard-cooked eggs
>
> 1 Tablespoon Dijon mustard

Mix all ingredients together and transfer to a $1^1/2$-quart casserole. Bake uncovered in 350°F oven for 25 to 30 minutes until heated through. Top each cracker with shredded Parmesan.

≈ PANDORA ≈

THE INQUIRING MIND

*One must still have chaos in one's life to be able to
give birth to a dancing star.*
—*Friedrich Nietzsche*

Pandora was totally set up by Zeus. He gave her the gift of curiosity and sent her off with a clay vessel to deliver to Epimetheus, telling her not to open it along the way. Zeus was offering the lovely Pandora to Epimetheus as a gift, something gods could get away with, apparently. Hera, Zeus' wife, overhears the plan and gives Pandora the gift of hope as well. She sensed some trickery afoot. Hera was hip to Zeus and his deception and meddling ways. Let's just say this wasn't the first time. Pandora opens the vessel, of course. Good girl. Evidently, the pot contained despair and dark notions, which were now let loose on the world. So once again, all evil can be blamed on women and their inquiring minds. All sounds very Garden of Eden to me. Thank goodness gal pal Hera added hope to the mix, counteracting the despair in the vessel.

From Pandora we remember to open every single jar, door, invitation, book, nook, and cranny that catches our fancy. We are here to try it all on for size, every adventure, encounter, and experience. Quieting a curious heart or mind is the greatest mishap, surely not indulging ignited passions or inquisitive insights.

FALLING DOWN

I use that expression all the time when something just blows me away—when someone says something lovely, or I see something beautiful or in a new way, or most anything nature offers up. It doesn't mean failing or losing it or stumbling—well maybe stumbling, but only because something knocks you off your feet in a good way. I used to literally fall down a lot, usually because I was wearing shoes like clogs that had a tendency to throw me to the ground on a regular basis. I still wear clogs or clog-esque shoes almost every day, but I may have learned how to walk in them a tad better or catch myself from falling a bit quicker.

Now I just figuratively fall down a lot. My falling down became a joke with my friends, though. While traveling with my friend Ann Marie in Portugal, we couldn't help snooping around in a palace trying to check out the fancy off-limits rooms. Off limits, please. Two uppity American women? Not a chance. Pandora was just screaming in our ears to keep searching for a way in. I had visions of Bluebeard's women or Mr. Rochester's

You Madame, Are a Fraud!

It is somehow reassuring to know that I am not the only one who suffers from the fraud syndrome. I just recently discovered that a very talented and smart actress said she has a fear of being revealed as a fraud. She thinks it is possible that someone is going to walk into her house and take away her diploma from an Ivy League college and her Academy Award. What each of us is afraid to be revealed as will be different and may change with time and circumstance. I have no scientific data to back this up, but I have never talked to a man who feels this way, only women. A man has never told me a story that starts out, "I was going into a big ➡

wife locked away behind each of the imposing carved wooden doors and was ready for anything. We thought we were being pretty clever and inconspicuous as we tiptoed through the hallways, rattling doorknobs. I'm not sure how successful we thought we could have been, seeing as we were on the verge of hysterical laughing fits from the beginning of the adventure. As we crept, or more appropriately, crashed along the corridor, I tried the heavy doorknob of the next room and suddenly it opened. I fell across the threshold and landed in a heap halfway

meeting and was deathly afraid of being revealed as a fraud. . . . "
Maybe they don't admit it. Who knows?

A mom friend of mine told me the other day that sometimes when she loses it and yells at her kids, she is convinced that the parenting police are going to storm her house at just that moment and point a dagger of a finger at her and say, "Aha! We knew it all along, you are a bad mother. Good mothers never lose it; they stay in control." Yikes. What an awful lot of extra stress to put on ourselves, but we do tend to fall into that trap. My women's group spent a whole evening discussing the fraud factor. It was very therapeutic and has sparked an ongoing discussion.

into the room. We both screamed and ran, or tried to and wept with laughter for hours. It still makes me smile a big grin, the memory of slapstick, ridiculous fun with my friend. I can't even say it happened when we were teenagers because we were both in our thirties. That is one of the parts I love best about the story.

We have to laugh with abandon all through life, not just when we are tiny young things and not always when it is deemed appropriate by others. I love the mischievous goofy side of me and my chums who love to giggle to the point of no return.

Isn't it just the best to laugh so hard that tears stream down your face, especially with a co-conspirator? Those are the times of great connection, when you are the only two in on the joke and nothing else matters. I think I would just about die if I couldn't laugh. Don't you think? I love falling down.

SEVEN THOUSAND BROKEN HEARTS

"I would rather experience seven thousand broken hearts than wake up every day thinking, 'Oh no, another day.'" I said that to a friend of mine who was trying to explain (justify) why he hadn't been in a relationship for a long time. He said that is was easier not giving love a try and not getting hurt, that is was inevitable he was going to experience or cause pain if he got involved with

Feeling Like a Cowgirl

I bought cowboy boots when I lived out West. I still have them and still wear them sometimes. When I put on my boots I feel pretty brave, pretty tough. I walk with a bit more ease out there in the world. I can belly up to the bar or to the line at the post office, doesn't much matter. I feel like someone worth reckoning with. Do you get a little confidence boost from something in your wardrobe? It's just good to know it's there. Something must make your soul swagger, just a bit? Come on now, fess up. Put it on and show yourself.

someone again. Easier?! Easier not to take the jump into connection and intimacy? Easier not to *feel* and love and give and receive the tornadoes of emotion and fantasy and anticipation? Oh, I don't think so. What is the point of life anyway? Isn't that why we are here, to experience everything and to crash around and to trip and soar and dance and weep? And more and more and more. It isn't about getting there (wherever there is). It isn't about anything being perfect. It is all about the trip and the falls and the stumbles and the steadying and the tipping over and the craning your neck out the car window like a big ol' dog and feeling the whole world on your face as you venture out. Unleash a little havoc, put the big emotions out there. It's the only way we figure out what it is that makes us giddy and full and wanting more.

GROUP CELEBRATION

★) ★

Wonderland

This is a great "getting to know you" activity and can easily be done over dinner. There are no supplies needed; just come with an open and inquisitive mind. It's time to find out a little bit more about each other. Do you know all the birthdays of the women in the group? What about favorite colors, movies,

★ Earning Your Pandora Badge ★

ON YOUR OWN: BIG YELLOW TAXI

The great thing about cabs in New York is that there are so many of them. They are like bees in a hive, buzzing and flying by everywhere. I love that you climb in and tell the driver a very precise address, down to the north or south corner of the street you are going to, and before you have even shut the door all the way the cab lurches forward like a wild horse with a mind of its own. I never have figured out when the driver has had time to figure out the best route there or which side street to try for a short cut. It must happen in a split second. The map of Manhattan is the cab driver's language. They know this menu by heart and then some, but I think the cabs are actually enchanted and drive themselves.

Try drawing a yellow taxicab like the famous NYC ones or make yours a London taxi or a Filipino jitney cab. Or buy a little one in a toy store. This cab can take you anywhere in the universe that you can conjure up in your imagination. Get in your mind or on paper and tell it where to go. See and describe everything you pass by. What does it smell like inside the cab and out? What time of year is it? Do you have the windows open in the cab? Is it day or night? How fast are you going? What is your driver like? Is anyone in the cab with you? Who is it? How long will they be riding with you? Allow Pandora's curious nature to fill you with color and questions and the scenery of your imagination and your dreams. What do you see? What do you want to see? Grab on tight to that strap above the door and head out. It is all about possibility, and only a cab ride away.

books, or foods? Where has each always wanted to travel? Who was their first crush? Spend time at dinner or afterward and ask questions. Maybe you will come up with a questionnaire that each new member will answer. You can put them in a book with a picture of each gal if you like or just keep asking new questions.

RECIPES FOR PANDORA

Chocolate Whiskey Truffles

These are melt-in-your-mouth delicious, and I have made them for several goddess feasts. Pandora should slip a few to Zeus next time he summons her with one of his great ideas.

> 8 oz. semisweet chocolate, chopped
>
> 1 stick unsalted butter
>
> $2/3$ cup crushed gingersnap cookies
>
> 3 Tablespoons whiskey (Jack Daniels works well.)
>
> $1/2$ cup unsweetened cocoa powder
>
> $1/2$ cup powdered sugar

Melt chocolate and butter in heavy medium saucepan over low heat, stirring until smooth. Mix in crushed cookies and whiskey. Pour into bowl. Cover and chill until firm, about 45 minutes.

Line cookie sheet with foil. Drop truffle mixture by tablespoons onto foil, spacing apart. Freeze 15 minutes. Roll each between palms of hands until smooth and round. Sift cocoa powder and sugar into shallow dish. Roll each truffle into cocoa mixture. Let stand 10 minutes before serving. They would go really well with the next recipe, too. Makes 20 to 24 truffles.

Vanilla Café Olé

Picture a snowy evening with all the gals gathered around the fire-place after a delicious meal. Here is a sumptuous way to add a dash more warmth to the night. Don't use skim or 2 percent milk, just doesn't work. This is a treat after all.

> 1 cup half-and-half
>
> 2 cups whole milk
>
> 3 cups hot brewed coffee
>
> 1 vanilla bean, split lengthwise
>
> Kahlua or other coffee-flavored liqueur, to taste

Combine the half-and-half, milk, and sugar in a saucepan. Scrape the seeds from the vanilla bean into the pan and also add the whole bean. Simmer over low heat for 20 minutes. Remove the vanilla bean and whisk briefly.

Fill mugs with ³/₄ cup coffee and ³/₄ cup milk mixture. Top with a few tablespoons (or more to taste) of liqueur. This is guaranteed to warm you to your toes. Serves 4, easily doubled or tripled!

THE WHOLE ENCHILADA

Here's the tricky part. You are the author of your own legend. You may think others have editing rights, but they don't unless you let them. So keep the big red pen away from everyone else. Many people may have interpretations of your myth, but the only one it really matters to is you. You are unlike every other being on this Earth, Miss Snowflake. Follow your own path in your own way. The grail *is* the path, the journey onward and inward. The treasure is your adventure, all that you can be and all that you can become and experience. Your journey will be like no other. Take every turn that catches your fancy. Look high, look low, pick things up and put them down. Admire the shiny poison ivy from a distance, or pack a lot of calamine lotion if you can't resist. Skip or run down the trail, crawl if you have to. Don't panic if you think you are lost, just make a new choice. You are never really off track. By the time you bend down to tie your shoes a little tighter and stand back up, the world will look a whole lot different. New paths will emerge. Pick one. Simple as that.

Every minute of every day you have the option of how

you want to show up in your life. Don't try living someone else's choices. It is not possible. Find your own road. Follow the scents you find intriguing, the colors that entice you, and the music from within. Your journey is the one that will lead you to happiness and delight, not one that has already been set down by others. It cannot be the same experience if you try and follow a path already taken anyway, so don't bother.

Sometimes you do have to buy the ruby slippers and walk around in them at home awhile before you tap dance on out into the world. That's just fine. Your life in Technicolor and the yellow brick road will be right outside your door whenever you decide to take a peek and put a sparkling toe to the ground.

You will be making everything up as you go along on this wild ride, but that is the source of the excitement and enlightenment. It has to be that way. There has never been another you. And there never will be again. Get it? Gather your gals, give them a wink, and check in when you need to. Time to bushwhack, ladies. It's a workout and it's why we're here. What are you waiting for? Permission?! Cue the music when you're ready and get on out there!

ABOUT THE AUTHOR

 Hailey D.D. Klein is a Usui and Tibetan Reiki Master, and Flower Essence Practitioner who creates rituals for clients and friends. The rituals are designed to offer guidance in living a life filled with curiosity, balance, and delight. She is a founding member of a goddess group that's still going strong after more than ten years of meeting and celebrating together. Additionally, Klein is a filmmaker who has worked in art departments producing feature films and corporate videos. She is also the author of *The Way of Change: Finding Joy in Your Journey*. Hailey lives in Massachusetts.

TO OUR READERS